"Workers and bosses have conflicting interests. Workers build power in the workplace. Unions need to strike to win. Strikes need to shut down the company. These are basic ideas that built the labor movement, but they have fallen out of favor in recent years. In this bracing call to action, Joe Burns calls for a revival of class struggle unionism, showing why it's the only hope for rebuilding the labor movement and creating a better world."

—**Barry Eidlin**, McGill University

"I appreciate theories about union organizing and socialism, but I always needed something I could carry back to work. Joe Burns did it again. He explains in prose as solid and precise as a toolmaker's what class struggle unionism is, how it works, and how to implement a workable solution to the chronic failure of socialist organizing: integration with the working class."

—**Gregg Shotwell**, author, *Autoworkers Under the Gun: A Shop-Floor View of the End of the American Dream*

"Joe Burns's new book, *Class Struggle Unionism*, is both timely and urgently needed for young and new fighters emerging in the labor movement today. It's also a must-read for those union veterans who need a shot of adrenaline after many years. Winning will come from disciplined efforts and adherence to proven formulas, not from employer schemes or panaceas dreamed up by those far, far away from our reality. I recommend it to all militants in the workplaces today trying to kickstart our movement again."

—**Chris Townsend**, organizing director of ATU International Union

"With the public's and particularly young people's growing support for unions, Joe Burns has written an easy-to-read and insightful contribution. *Class Struggle Unionism* clarifies the different approaches to labor organizing and contract campaigns, staff roles and responsibilities, and, most importantly, different philosophies of labor's vision and mission. Burns's prescriptions for the labor movement's revitalization build on his own years of practical experience. Anyone who aspires to be a union leader or organizer should read this book!"

—**Rand Wilson**, former national or

"Written in a very accessible fashion, this book provides a refreshingly bold, uncompromising, and compelling reassertion of the value of the class struggle and need for a form of 'kick-ass,' fighting unionism, fundamentally different from what we are accustomed to today within the labor movement. It deserves to become an A-Z guidebook for activists in helping to energize collective resistance."

—**Ralph Darlington**, emeritus professor of employment relations, University of Salford

"Can the union movement revive, or even survive, without winning more fights against corporate power? Joe Burns doesn't think so. In *Class Struggle Unionism*, Burns makes the case for labor organizations that are militant, democratic, and membership-oriented. Drawing on his own past experience in the public and private sector, Burns provides a road map for union rebuilding that will increase bargaining and organizing success. His latest invaluable book is essential reading for rank-and-file activists, new and old."

—**Steve Early**, author, *Refinery Town* and *Civil Wars in US Labor*

"Joe Burns's *Class Struggle Unionism* has application to working-class struggles around the world. This book shows we can address the challenges of class struggle unionism, which are capable of defeating our ruling classes. Our organizing task is historic, necessary, and urgent in today's capitalist domination, exploitation, and ecological crisis."

—**Chris White**, former secretary of the United Trades and Labor Council of South Australia

"In *Class Struggle Unionism*, Joe Burns makes an impassioned argument for a militant labor movement. He covers a great deal of ground in this highly readable volume that challenges contemporary unions to step out of their complacency to build a more just and equitable world."

—**Tom Juravich**, professor of labor studies, University of Massachusetts Amherst

"In this new book, *Class Struggle Unionism*, written and published just as pundits and labor activists are hailing the resurgence of strikes, militancy, and new organizing, Joe Burns fires a well-aimed volley across the bow of 'business unionism' and 'labor liberalism,' insisting that

Praise for *Class Struggle Unionism*

"There is nothing more essential for the resurgence of the labor movement than to cut through the racial, social, gender, and political divisions driven by the corporate class to deny the working class power and keep workers in competition with each other. *Class Struggle Unionism* not only defines the urgency of our common struggle, it's a textbook on how to organize around our common demands right where we work in order to build a movement strong enough to realize an inclusive economy and thriving democracy. This is required reading for these times, and required consciousness for our labor movement at all times."

—**Sara Nelson**, international president of the Association of Flight Attendants, CWA

"Anyone trying to rebuild an effective US labor movement needs to read *Class Struggle Unionism* by Joe Burns. He lays out the fundamental principles that UE has tried to uphold for the last eighty-five years. For a union to be worthwhile to the working class, it needs to know which side it is on, and it has to recognize that the fight itself is what allows workers to gain the knowledge and power they need."

—**Carl Rosen**, general president of United Electrical Workers (UE)

"Joe Burns's *Class Struggle Unionism* gives us a vision of what a labor movement should and could be. Burns reminds us that unions are about more than collective bargaining. When workers take collective action into their own hands, they can change the political agenda and bring real power to the struggles for equality and a truly democratic society."

—**Kim Moody**, author, *On New Terrain: How Capital Is Shaping the Battleground of Class War*

"What will reignite the labor movement? Beyond organizing techniques, *Class Struggle Unionism* argues that a revival would require a grounding in class struggle ideology and organizing to name and confront the power of capital. Burns draws out why this has gone missing from labor, the steps to bring it back, and the solidarity and power it will build. Read it. Share it. Put the movement back in the labor movement."

—**Barbara Madeloni**, Labor Notes, former president of Massachusetts Teachers Association

"*Class Struggle Unionism* has arrived just in time. It is supremely relevant and cutting-edge smart, providing exactly what's needed at a moment when our labor movement is finally regaining its footing after decades of flat-footed, directionless wandering. Joe Burns thinks strategically like an organizer, brings the sweeping view of a historian, and writes so that workers, organizers, and allies can come away transformed by what he says. It is a book that reminds us why we have a labor movement, and what hell we can raise when we remember which side we're on."

—**Ellen David Friedman**, Labor Notes

"How can we rekindle widespread working-class militancy? And what should such militancy seek to achieve? In *Class Struggle Unionism*, Joe Burns makes the case that a combative, cohesive, and effective labor movement requires class-conscious unions expressly committed to challenging capitalist exploitation. Burns's handbook will prove invaluable to organizers who recognize that taking on the ruling class must begin with an ideological reorientation of the labor movement."

—**Toni Gilpin**, author, *The Long Deep Grudge: A Story of Big Capital, Radical Labor, and Class War in the American Heartland*

"Joe Burns's *Class Struggle Unionism* is a must-read for any labor activists or socialists concerned with the future of the US workers' movement. He details that the ersatz social unionism of "labor liberalism"—with its abandonment of workplace organization and struggle and reliance on professional staff and alliances with the Democratic Party—is no alternative to the discredited "business unionism" that had dominated US labor since World War II. His alternative—a class struggle unionism that builds upon workplace confrontations to challenge capitalist exploitation and oppression across society—is crucial for labor militants today."

—**Charlie Post**, editor of *Spectre: A Marxist Journal*

"The notion of 'class struggle unionism' sounds like 'duh' until you realize how widespread is the idea that some force can save workers other than workers themselves—in *Class Struggle Unionism*, Joe Burns has coined the great phrase 'labor liberalism,' and makes clear why the labor movement can't survive without committing to fighting the bosses and thinking big."

—**Jane Slaughter**, Labor Notes

'class struggle unionism' provides a path leading not only to the revival of the labor movement but also to the transformation of the American working class into a cohesive force for social change. *Class Struggle Unionism* is certain to become part of the brewing debates among labor activists, scholars, socialist theorists, and union supporters as we seek to learn from history, think critically about the present, and envision a brighter future."

—**Peter Rachleff**, co-executive director of East Side
Freedom Library, St. Paul, Minnesota

"How are we going to build a movement that can occupy plants, violate injunctions, and pick the big, audacious fights that will galvanize millions of workers? Joe Burns shows how the only answer is a movement grounded in a clear understanding of the struggle between workers and bosses. We don't need more labor-management partnership, better tactics, or more polished messaging. We need a labor movement that stands for militant struggle, member control, antiracism, and political independence—and isn't afraid to say it. Joe Burns offers some of the vital tools we'll need to get there."

—**Mark Meinster**, director of organization
of United Electrical Workers (UE)

CLASS STRUGGLE UNIONISM

Joe Burns

Haymarket Books
Chicago, Illinois

Published in 2022 by
Haymarket Books
P.O. Box 180165
Chicago, IL 60618
773-583-7884
www.haymarketbooks.org
info@haymarketbooks.org

ISBN: 978-1-64259-584-0

Distributed to the trade in the US through Consortium Book Sales and Distribution (www.cbsd.com) and internationally through Ingram Publisher Services International (www.ingramcontent.com).

This book was published with the generous support of Lannan Foundation and Wallace Action Fund.

Special discounts are available for bulk purchases by organizations and institutions. Please call 773-583-7884 or email info@haymarketbooks.org for more information.

Cover design by Eric Kerl.

Printed in Canada by union labor.

Library of Congress Cataloging-in-Publication data is available.

10 9 8 7 6 5 4 3 2 1

To Melissa

Contents

Introduction

To revive the labor movement, we need to revive class struggle unionism. Class struggle unionism is a form of unionism that challenges the control over our society by the superrich—the handful of billionaires who own the vast majority of resources in the United States and the world. Every part of class struggle unionism, from the guiding ideas to strike tactics to organizing techniques, is shaped by an understanding of this class struggle.

For one hundred years up until the 1990s, class struggle unionism was the main alternative to bureaucratic business unionism. The dividing line between business unionism and class struggle unionism was simple: whether you accepted the very right of management to exploit labor of working people. The business unionists said sure, as long as they got a "fair day's pay for a fair day's work," they would accept management's control of the workplace and the economy. Class struggle unionists said no, "labor creates all wealth," and viewed their unionism as one part of a bigger struggle against the billionaire class.

In the coming chapters we will discuss how billionaires are created. Understanding why and how billionaires exist leads to a very distinct and complete framework of unionism. Class struggle unionism as a philosophy aims big, for the abolition of the billionaire class. As such, it rejects a small-ball approach to union issues. Class struggle unionists believe in militancy, shop floor struggle, union democracy, fighting the system, and prioritizing antiracist struggle.

Class struggle unionism is responsible for some of the brightest moments in labor history. It motivated the Industrial Workers of the World in their brand of revolutionary unionism, which contributed to some of the greatest strikes in US history. The great socialist leader Eugene Debs moved from conservative railroad business unionism to socialism through participation in class struggle. The key militants in the great strikes of 1934 in Minneapolis, Toledo, and the West Coast were class struggle unionists. Adherents built a civil rights unionism in the US South following World War II.

One of the key weaknesses of the labor movement since the early 1990s is the absence of a broad-based, explicit class struggle union trend. When I entered the labor movement in the 1980s, I got the tail end of such a trend. Coming out of the great upsurges of the 1960s—the civil rights, antiwar, and women's movements—thousands of socialists joined the labor movement, explicitly adopting a class struggle union framework. It drove unionists to ground themselves in rank-and-file unionism, bringing us enduring institutions such as Teamsters for a Democratic Union, Labor Notes, Black Workers for Justice, and many other rank-and-file-oriented institutions.

I will argue in this book that for the first time in US labor history, class struggle unionism has been eclipsed as the main alternative to business unionism, replaced by an approach that I call labor liberalism. While this approach focuses on organizing techniques and ties to the community, it lacks critical components of class struggle unionism, including a willingness to challenge the union bureaucracy, shop floor militancy, rank-and-file democracy, and an overall opposition to the system of capitalism.

We need to have a sober assessment of the situation we face and our prospects going forward. We are getting our asses kicked. Only six out of a hundred private-sector workers belong to unions. Most major industries such as trucking, residential construction, retail, and finance are virtually non-union. Where remnants of unionism do exist, such as meatpacking, the established unions are bureaucratic and ineffectual. Our contracts have been decimated, and once-strong pensions and health-care programs have been gutted. Optimism only goes so far, and at some point realism needs to take hold.

Let's be honest. We have no plan to revive the labor movement. For several decades, we have attempted to revive unionism within a political and legal system set up to benefit the billionaire class. It's not working. The owners of industry take in billions and billions of profits, creating a class of people with unimaginable economic and political power. Money is power. For unionists, this power shapes our unionism in more ways than we care to admit.

In my previous books, *Reviving the Strike* and *Strike Back*, I looked back to labor history to argue that we need to revive the strike. I argued that in both the 1930s for private workers and the 1960s for public-sector workers, the strike was the indispensable tactic that helped win our unions. Here, likewise, we can look to labor history to demonstrate the power of a unionism shaped by class struggle principles.

Those of us who want a militant, democratic, antiracist, antisexist, and fighting labor movement have a choice. Piecemeal reform is not going to work. Our unionism must become a lot more bold, a lot more radical, a lot more strategic, and a lot less willing to accept the status quo. We need a new framework.

Over my thirty-plus years of labor activism and bargaining, I have found inspiration from working people coming together to strike back against management. Today, there are signs of hope. In recent years we have witnessed teachers in states such as West Virginia, Oklahoma, and Arizona striking statewide and the growth of pro-working-class politics represented by the Bernie Sanders campaigns and the growth of the Democratic Socialists of America. We have millions of youth taking to the streets to demand Black Lives Matter.

We have an opportunity to build a new type of labor movement. But we cannot build it based on the tired ideas of the last three decades. The billionaire class is powerful, organized, and vicious. To take them on we need our own philosophy—class struggle unionism.

Chapter 1

Shop Floor Economics

Class struggle unionism places our union struggles as part of a larger struggle between the two major classes in society, the working class and the owning class (also called the 1 percent or the billionaire class). Rather than taking on individual bad employers, class struggle unionists fight the entire class of billionaires who control our economy and our government. For that reason, our discussion must begin with an analysis of these two basic classes in society.

Working people are the vast majority of the population. Working people are truck drivers, clerical workers, baristas, restaurant workers, teachers, nurses, carpenters, and autoworkers. The working class holds little income-producing wealth and must work for others in order to get by. A relative handful belong to unions, but almost 90 percent work in non-union workplaces.

Professor Michael Zweig includes in the working class

> those people with relatively little power at work—white-collar bank tellers, call-center workers, and cashiers; blue-collar machinists, construction workers, and assembly-line workers; pink-collar secretaries, nurses, and home-health workers—skilled and unskilled, men and women of all races, nationalities, and sexual preferences. The working class are those with little personal control over the pace or content of their work and without supervisory control over the work lives of others.[1]

The defining feature of the working class is that members must sell their labor to others to survive. For most folks, it is taken for granted that in order to pay our rent and put food on the table, we must go out and get a job. Although workers may own some personal property such as cars or even houses, working-class people hold little in the way of income-producing property like factories, businesses, stocks, and commercial real estate.

There is, though, another group in society that by virtue of owning stocks and other property would not have to work another day in their lives. This group of people, the billionaires and multimillionaires, own the stocks, businesses, and properties that produce income. They make money not by working themselves but by having others work for them.

The billionaire class controls most of the income-producing wealth in the United States and the world. Three individuals, Jeff Bezos, Bill Gates, and Warren Buffett, own more wealth than half the population of the United States. Every year, *Forbes* magazine covers the top four hundred richest people in the US. In 2020, the average net worth on the list was $8 billion.[2] A billion dollars is a lot of money, more than we might think. As economist Michael Yates points out, "If a person spent $10,000 per day . . . it would take 100,000 days to spend a billion dollars, just under 274 years."[3] So the average billionaire on the *Forbes* list could spend ten grand a day for two thousand years.

These are the superrich. Traditionally, folks who owned industry were called capitalists because they controlled the income-producing capital in society, along with the CEOs and top managers of business. Lately folks have called them the 1 percent or the billionaire class. Understanding how and why billionaires are created is the first step in establishing class struggle unionism.

How Are Billionaires Created?

Appropriately enough for a book on unionism, our analysis begins in the workplace. Think of your workplace. It could be a hospital, a factory, or a restaurant. During your shift you pour lattes or weld metal or care for patients. You provide services, build things, or make, transport, or sell products.

What you have in common with one another is that you take the materials provided and make something more of them. During your shift you expend physical or mental labor, and in the process, goods or services are produced that are more valuable because of your labor. Nurses provide nursing care. Amazon workers distribute goods. Autoworkers build cars. In return you get an hourly wage or perhaps a salary.

The owners are the investment funds or billionaires who own the stock in the company. They supply the building, machinery, and raw materials. They hire workers and control the physical and intellectual property of the business. They hire supervisors and managers. But despite their ownership of the enterprise, they often have very little to do with the business. They may never have set foot onto the property and certainly do not supply the physical or mental energy to power the company.

Despite their lack of connection to the workplace, the owners keep the product of the workers' labor that they sell to consumers. Now, this state of affairs is accepted as just the way things are, the natural order of the universe, or the "free market." Employers are considered to have invested in the business, taken the risk, or even created the company. Under this framework workers are hired to do a job and receive wages in return, and they have no more stake in the final product than any other supplier into the production process. Human labor is treated just like any other raw material or input into production.

This employment transaction is rarely questioned. But why is that the case? The owners did not do the work. You and your co-workers did all the work. Nor did the employer create any of the inputs into the production process. They did not themselves build the buildings, grow the coffee beans, make the tools you use, or assemble the trucks you drive. Other groups of workers, who are similarly exploited, created the inputs supposedly supplied by the owners.

Billionaires say they deserve the billions because they are the creators of the business. This is wrong for several reasons. Billionaires do not create new industries or businesses by themselves. New industries are social creations utilizing technology created by scientists, researchers, and inventors, often with significant government funding. Jeff Bezos, the billionaire of Amazon, explains that a big part of his success came from the efforts of others:

> How did that happen in such a short period of time? It happened because we didn't have to do any of the heavy lifting. All of the heavy-lifting infrastructure was already in place for it. There was already a telecommunication network, which became the backbone of the internet. There was already a payment system—it was called the credit card. There was already a transportation network called the US Postal Service, and Royal Mail, and Deutsche Post, all over the world, that could deliver our packages.[4]

Steven Jobs did not create computer science, and Mark Zuckerberg did not create the internet. They built their fortunes by assuming control over emerging and existing industries.

When you think about it this way, it is not really ownership that determines who gets to keep the surplus produced during the work shift; it's about control over resources. The billionaire class gets to keep the surplus produced because they have power and control over the productive wealth of society. Productive wealth is income-producing wealth such as ownership of businesses, buildings, and stocks and bonds. Traditionally, class struggle unionists refer to the income-producing businesses, factories, and other investments as the *means of production*.

As Michael Parenti explained in his 1970s book *Democracy for the Few*, "You are a member of the owning class when your income is very large and comes mostly from the labor of other people, that is, when others work for you, either in a company you own, or by creating the wealth that allows your investments to give you a handsome return. The secret to wealth is not to work hard but to have others work hard for you."[5]

The means of production are incredibly concentrated. Many of us have some limited personal wealth such as a car or a house if we're lucky. But that is not wealth that can produce income; it is simply to live and survive. The top 1 percent own half of the stocks and the top 10 percent own 92 percent of all stocks, meaning the bottom 90 percent of people in the US own just 8 percent of stocks.[6] As my dear mother used to say, "Those that gots, gets."

A French economist named Thomas Piketty caused a stir in elite circles in 2014 when he produced a massive book titled *Capital in the Twenty-First Century*. Analyzing years of data, he showed that wealth inequality was at record highs and that it was going to keep getting more extreme. According to Piketty, the reason is simple: "When the rate of return on capital significantly exceeds the growth rate of the economy . . . then it logically follows that inherited wealth grows faster than output and income."[7]

Simply put, the more wealth you have the more wealth you accumulate in a never-ending spiral.

Accumulated wealth does not sit still. It must seek out new opportunities for exploitation. One hundred years ago it prompted the European powers to divide up the globe into colonies to provide markets and cheap labor for an ever-expanding economic system. Capital flows into new businesses and industries, upending labor relations. This accumulated capital is a relentless force.

By and large, union leaders are not big on change. Business unionists love procedures—the grievance procedures and stable collective bargaining. But stability is an illusion. And they are paralyzed in the face of chaos. Yet, for decades we as a labor movement have acted as if we want to simply go back to the past—to reset the rules on union organizing. It's not happening.

This constant drive to the bottom means for unions it's kill or be killed. Our unionism is in constant battle with the employer class, punctuated by temporary truces. But class struggle unionists believe our unionism must break this vicious cycle and fight for an economy where workers control the wealth we create. To do that, however, requires a deeper understanding of how billionaires separate workers from the wealth they create.

The Separation of Workers from Wealth

Big Bill Haywood, the silver miner who became a leader of the Industrial Workers of the World in the early 1900s, noted, "The mine owners did not find the gold. They did not mine the gold, they did not mill the gold, but by some weird alchemy all the gold belonged to them!" As Haywood noted, although workers produce all goods and services, the outcome of the work process is to make a handful of people rich and most poor. Understanding how this happens requires looking at the employment process differently from what we have been fed our entire lives.

For working-class youth, it is taken for granted that once you reach a certain age, it is your individual responsibility to get a job and work for another sixty years or more until you retire. You do that by being hired by an employer who hires you for a set rate per hour. In exchange your employer controls your time and method of work.

Now, if you are one of the lucky ones to have a union contract in place, your pay may be marginally higher, and the contract may place some limitations on the power of the employer. But under most union contracts the right of management to direct the workforce is generally accepted. Regardless, the owners keep the surplus produced, and the essence of the wage transaction does not change.

But let's examine this transaction a bit closer. Let's say you get hired for $20 an hour. This is treated as a contractual transaction just like millions of others that occur each day. No different than a consumer buying eggs at the grocery store or corporations buying tons of steel to build cars. The employer hires you to work and pays you for your capacity to work.

For an eight-hour shift, your earnings would be $160, but with fringe benefits (vacation, health, social security), let's say the total outlay is $200. The proportionate share of the materials, cost of machinery, rent, and overhead is another $300 during that shift. This means the employer has spent a total of $500 for the cost of your labor, materials, and overhead.

During your shift, however, your labor transforms the raw materials into something more. Otherwise there would be no point in hiring you. Let's say that after the employer has sold goods that you produced, the total value realized by the employer is $800 attributable for the work during your shift. Once the $500 is subtracted, the remaining $300 is kept by the employer. The billionaires call this profit. Class struggle unionists call it theft.

Wages Paid During Shift	$160
Fringe Benefits	$40
Additional Employer Costs	$300
Total Cost per Shift	$500
Value Produced	$800
Difference Kept	$300

An alternative way to look at this is that the employer makes enough to pay your wages in five hours, and for the remaining three hours you would be working for free. Your pay is a fraction of the total value added during your shift. That difference is the key to everything, the source of power and privilege of the rich in society and why we have billionaires.

Of course, the reality is more complicated than this example. Folks rarely work alone and often work in giant enterprises with hundreds or thousands of workers. So one has to perform this calculation on a broader basis, but the analysis is no less correct. One can do this on a snapshot basis by looking at the total bottom line of the employer. As one journalist explained,

> In this account, all the revenue that a business takes in is produced by its employees, who manufacture the company's wares and/or provide its services. That revenue, minus the expense of raw materials, tools, utilities, etc., equals the value that the employees have created using those raw materials, tools, utilities, etc. Rather than receiving the full value of their work, though, employees are given only a relatively small proportion of it as wages, while the employer keeps the rest.[8]

It does not matter in what industry one works, the basic calculation is the same.

Let's use Amazon as a real-world example. Amazon has hundreds of thousands of employees working all across the globe.

> During the third quarter of 2018, Amazon made nearly $1 billion a month in profit. Were it distributed equally between its roughly 500,000 employees, each employee would earn an extra $2,000 a month. That's quite the bonus, considering that most Amazon employees, if they work full time, earn a little more than $2,400 a month even *after* their recently hard-won fight for $15 an hour.
>
> Instead, that $1 billion-a-month profit goes to Amazon leadership and gets distributed according to the whim of its board of directors—of which Bezos is the chairman."[9]

So in this example, workers at Amazon would be getting paid somewhat less than half of the value they collectively produce. The remainder flows upward to the owners of the enterprise, making Jeff Bezos the richest person on the planet.

Now, employers work very hard to disguise this unequal relationship. For good reason. If it were clear that a class of people was stealing four hours a day from people, that would cause a scandal. But that is not how they talk about it. It's in the interest of employers to obscure labor's role as the producer of wealth in society.

In the mid-1800s, when the system of capitalism was emerging, a theorist named Karl Marx sought to explain its workings. Marx compared the differences between the old system where peasants worked for feudal lords with the new system of working for wages:

> In point of fact, however, whether a man works three days of the week for himself on his own field and three days for nothing on the estate of his lord, or whether he works in the factory or the workshop six hours daily for himself and six for his employer, comes to the same, although in the latter case the paid and unpaid portions of labour are inseparably mixed up with each other, and the nature of the whole transaction is completely masked by the *intervention of a contract* and the *pay* received at the end of the week. The gratuitous labour appears to be voluntarily given in the

one instance, and to be compulsory in the other. That makes all the difference.[10]

What Marx was pointing out is that by calling the transaction a contract and making it appear totally voluntary, it really obscured the fact that part of the labor expended by workers was being taken by the owners of industry.

This analysis is the starting point of class struggle unionism. If one accepts this wage transaction at face value, then our job as unionists is merely to try to help workers sell their labor at the highest price possible. But under that framework, once the sale is complete, the right of employers to manage the workforce is not contested, and neither is their complete and absolute control over the business and profits. Traditionally those unionists who accept this inequality as just the way it is were traditionally referred to as "pure and simple trade unionists," or business unionists.

Class struggle unionists, by contrast, question this entire framework. Why do those who do not produce the work get to keep all of the value created? Workers spend a good portion of their waking hours at work, so why should they not be treated like free people? Or as labor's anthem "Solidarity Forever" points out, if "it is we who plowed the prairies; built the cities where they trade," then why do "we stand outcast and starving midst the wonders we have made"?

In the preceding pages I've focused mostly on workers for private-sector employers. But it's also necessary to point out the role of government workers as an important part of the working class and labor movement. Millions of union members work for government employers, including teachers, bus drivers, office workers, and many other working-class occupations. They are exploited, but the form of the exploitation is a bit different from private-sector workers.

Government workers provide the infrastructure for the economy in which the billionaires make their wealth, in addition to educating a workforce who can then be exploited, among other functions. The billionaires try to drive down the cost of public workers, so they can pay less in taxes, so they pocket more of the social surplus. Although government workers do not directly work for the billionaires, the concepts in this book, including those in chapter 2, fully apply.

Class Struggle

In *Solidarity Divided*, longtime labor activists Bill Fletcher and Fernando Gapasin explain how the division of society into two groups— the workers who produce things and the billionaires who take the product of labor—forms the basis for a struggle between classes.

> Class struggle emerges from a simple dynamic: in a society with a social surplus and a division between those who produce and those who make decisions, a struggle inevitably occurs over that surplus. Insofar as the surplus ultimately results from the uncompensated labor power of works and those workers—whether working or rendered "redundant"—have no say over the disposition of that surplus, an antagonism develops between those who possess the means of distributing that surplus (and thus hold power) and those who do not: those with the means to distribute the surplus ultimately control society's means of production, distribution, and exchange.[11]

Under this viewpoint, our unionism is part and parcel of a larger battle within society between the working class and the billionaire class.

Mainstream economic theory treats workers and owners as engaged in economic transactions as equals. But as economist and labor educator Michael Yates points out, "The two parties, capital and labor, do not face each other as equals, but as superior to inferior. One owns the workplace; the other has no choice but to labor for capital, if not in this workplace then in another."[12]

While conventional business unionists see a limited role for unions in negotiating improvements, class struggle unionists understand that we must challenge the very basis of this unequal system.

Viewing our union struggles as part of this basic conflict in society produces a fundamentally different form of unionism from what we are accustomed to today. Class struggle unionists see billion-aires not as simply the megarich, but a class of people who live off the labor of other people. This difference is not of income inequality but a different power relationship in society. Just as in old times there were feudal lords and peasants, slave owners and enslaved people, today there are business owners and workers.

Once we begin to see society divided into classes with mutual-ly opposed interests, our union world starts looking a lot different. Rather than fighting for scraps, we are fighting for what is rightfully ours. Rather than just fighting for a fair wage, we are fighting for control of our workplaces, of the wealth we create, and for our class in general. Our workplace struggles are part of a larger fight in soci-ety over the distribution of the social surplus.

But class is not the only division within society. Black workers have long suffered systematic racism in society both in and out of the workplace. Likewise women workers contend with sexism on the job and an unequal burden in housework and child-rearing. In our worldwide economy, immigrant workers are confined to the worst jobs, and workers around the world suffer horrible conditions.

Now to some, these forms of discrimination are merely about workers having misguided ideas, which lead them to discriminate. But racism and sexism stem from the basic elements of the eco-nomic system. The entire modern system of capitalism was built upon the stolen labor from slaves that provided the surplus for the great modernization known as the industrial revolution. As Karl Marx noted, slavery was key to the establishment of the modern economic system:

> Direct slavery is as much the pivot upon which our present-day industrialism turns as are machinery, credit, etc. Without slavery there would be no cotton, without cotton there would be no mod-ern industry. It is slavery that has given value to the colonies, it is the colonies that have created world trade, and world trade is the necessary condition for large-scale machine industry.... Slavery is therefore an economic category of paramount importance.[13]

With the defeat of the Confederacy in the United States Civil War in the late 1860s, employers continued to use white supremacy to destroy the solidarity of Black and white workers. Employers consciously used white supremacy in building a racial caste system where access to jobs, housing, and education was based on the color of skin.

Likewise, oppression based on gender is baked into the economic system. This takes the form of discrimination in job markets where women's work has long paid less than men's work. But it is rooted in the unequal division of unpaid labor in housework and raising children.

Any analysis of class struggle that fails to account for and struggle against these forms of oppression is incomplete and bound to fail. In coming chapters we will discuss how having an antiracist, antisexist, pro-immigrant stance must be at the core of class struggle unionism.

Chapter 2

Class Struggle Union Ideas

Vermont senator and 2016 and 2020 presidential candidate Bernie Sanders frequently answers questions by saying we need a political revolution. By this Sanders means that we need to be willing to take on the billionaire class that dominates our society: "To be successful in creating a government and economy that works for the many, we will have to take on powerful special interests that dominate our economic and political life. . . . These special interests have extraordinary power, and they will spend enormous sums of money to maintain the status quo and their wealth."[1]

Sanders sees his political efforts as part of a sustained and targeted mobilization against the billionaire class. Now, whether you agree with him or how much effort we should put into political campaigns, the point here is, to take on the billionaire class, we need to take on the political and economic establishment.

Likewise, we need a labor revolution. Our unionism must be fully integrated within the struggle between the working class and the billionaire class. Not in a "let's talk about this once a year in our labor education training" sort of way, but in a defining feature of our unionism way. From our core ideas to our union tactics and strategy to our organizing methods, all aspects of our unionism need to be based on the idea that ours is a struggle between opposing classes. Once unionists reject the idea that billionaires should be controlling our economy and setting labor policy, a whole new world opens up.

Luckily for us, the labor movement has a rich history of class struggle unionism. From the early socialist ideas that animated mainstream American Federation of Labor unionists such as the young Samuel Gompers and Peter McGuire, to ideas guiding the revolutionary Industrial Workers of the World, to the communists and socialists who built a militant and inclusive labor movement in the 1930s, we have a rich labor history to draw on.

When we look at class struggle unionists from previous generations, we see that on certain major questions they shared similar thoughts. This does not mean they agreed on everything, and in fact often they spent more time arguing with each other than they did with the bosses. But there is a coherent set of ideas, which can be called a class struggle ideology. These ideas, which we will discuss next, all flow from the economic discussion of the previous chapter.

Class Struggle Unionism
versus Business Unionism

Before discussing the specifics of class struggle unionism, we need to examine its main competitor, business unionism. Business unionists have a very narrow perspective, seeing the problem as that of individual workers versus bad employers who have too much power. Under this model, since the employment transaction is not disputed as inherently exploitative, business unionists focus on what workers should get paid and what modest limitations should be placed on employers. They do not challenge the existence of the billionaire class.

Business unionism has a long history in the US labor movement. As the convention of the International Trade Association of Hat Finishers of America resolved in 1854, "We are fully alive to the fact that the interests of both employers and employees are identical and we declare and acknowledge their right to manage and control their business as they see fit but at the same time claim for ourselves as a body the privilege of agreement upon any concerted action whereby our interests as mechanics shall not be injured."[2]

Business unionism sees disputes as narrowly defined between employees of a given firm and their managers.

Whereas class struggle unionists see themselves as fighting for all members of the working class, business unionists narrowly represent their members even when they are at odds with the broader working-class interests. Way back in 1914, Robert Hoxie defined business unionism as expressing

> the viewpoint and interests of the workers in a craft or industry rather than those of the working class as a whole. It aims chiefly at more here and now for the organized workers of the craft or industry, in terms mainly of higher wages, shorter hours, and better working conditions, regardless for the most part of the welfare of the workers outside the particular organic group, and regardless in general of political and social considerations except in so far as these bear directly upon its own economic ends. It is conservative in the sense that it professes belief in natural rights and accepts as inevitable, if not as just, the existing capitalistic organization and the wage system as well as existing property rights and the binding force of contract.[3]

Historically, while class struggle unionists demanded abolition of exploitation and believed labor creates all wealth, business unionists raised the far more limited slogan of "A fair day's wages for a fair day's work."

While business unionism was challenged by the IWW and by the left unions of the 1920s and 1930s, it emerged from the post–World War II period as the dominant form of unionism. Today it is the overwhelming form of unionism, with both conservative varieties (building trades, for example) and liberal varieties (the Service Employees International Union and many public employee unions, for example).

Like any set of ideas, business unionism does not spring from thin air. It is based in the reality that many union leaders and staff live different lives than the workers they represent. No longer working on the shop floor, they are under constant pressure from employers and the government to compromise. Business unionism is a stable philosophy that suits their interests—as opposed to class struggle unionism, which promotes conflict with employers, which could threaten the livelihoods of union leaders and staff. More discussion of business unionism follows in the next chapter, but here we will cover the main features of class struggle unionism. All of the concepts below, and in the coming chapters, extend from the fundamental point, discussed in the last chapter, that while workers create all wealth, the fruits of their labor flow to a relative handful of billionaires. Recognizing our unionism as part of a larger struggle between classes, and against exploitation, leads to a distinctive type of unionism.

Them and Us

Seeing the wage transaction as theft leads class struggle unionists to view our unions locked in constant battle with employers. Class struggle unionists, rather than seeing our worker-owner relationship as primarily cooperative but with occasional flare-ups, recognize that conflict is baked into an economic system that pits the interests of the working class against the employing class. This leads class struggle unionists to create a combative form of unionism that places sharp demands on employers and promotes rank-and-file activism.

Teamsters Local 574 under left-wing leadership conducted one of the most militant general strikes in US history, the 1934 Minneapolis truckers' strike. During this strike, truck drivers in Minneapolis fought the police, shut the entire city down, and won unionization for hundreds of workers. Local 574 went on to spur unionization of truck drivers in the upper Midwest.

On the heels of the 1934 Minneapolis truckers' strike, the class struggle militants wrote a new preamble to the Local 574 bylaws:

> The working class whose life depends on the sale of labor and the employing class who live upon the labor of others, confront each other on the industrial field contending for the wealth created by those who toil. The drive for profit dominates the bosses' life.

> Low wages, long hours, the speed-up are weapons in the hands of
> the employer under the wage system. . . . It is the natural right of
> all labor to own and enjoy the wealth created by it.[4]

This one short paragraph contains many of the concepts of class struggle unionism, all stemming from the economic analysis discussed in the previous chapter.

This preamble reflected a core value of class struggle unionism—the idea that labor and capital are locked in a battle, confronting each other on the industrial field. But it also contends that we are fighting to retain "wealth created by those who toil." This framework sets up an inescapable battle between those who exploit and those who produce. Finally, the preamble ties in the direct workplace concerns of the workers with the relentless greed of employers. As will be discussed in the rest of this chapter, this is a distinguishing characteristic of class struggle unionism.

Similarly, Big Bill Haywood's speech at the founding of the Industrial Workers of the World proclaimed, "This organization will be formed, based and founded on the class struggle, having in view no compromise and no surrender, and but one object and one purpose and that is to bring the workers of this country into the possession of the full value of the product of their toil."[5]

Whereas class struggle unionists promote class struggle, business unionists seek to avoid it. Business unionists value their relationship with management, often identify with company concerns, and consider themselves more pragmatic than the workers. That's not to say they won't struggle or get into bitter strikes, but overall they tend to view these as fights against unreasonable employers.

The title of this subsection comes from the classic labor book *Them and Us: Struggles of a Rank-and-File Union* by United Electrical, Radio and Machine Workers of America (UE) activists James J. Matles and James Higgins.[6] The book chronicles the UE's journey as a class struggle union, formed in the battles of the 1930s. UE was one of the eleven left-led unions that after World War II came into conflict with the government, corporate America, and business unionism. Fiercely democratic and contesting management at every turn, UE offers a different brand of organization even today. *Them and Us* captures the essence of UE's brand of class struggle unionism. Core to UE's belief, and indeed to all class struggle unionists, is the idea that we are locked in relentless battle with employers.

Understanding that our unionism is a struggle between workers and owners should be considered the cardinal principle of class struggle unionism. It is a simple idea that provides quite practical advice to guide our labor work:

- Understand that powerful financial interests are lined up against our unions.
- Understand that agreements with employers are temporary truces rather than alignment of interests.
- Understand that we have opposing interests on every issue.
- See ours as a struggle between classes.

The concept of us versus them is at the core of class struggle unionism.

In contrast, business unionists see workers' interests as aligned with those of employers. Having accepted the narrow framework of the wage transaction, business unionists tie the fate of workers to the success or failure of the firms they work for. Rather than believing labor creates all wealth, they accept the general framework that the employer controls the workplace and the fruits of labor. This forces us to negotiate from a position of weakness against an employing class that is constantly amassing greater power.

Business unionists often see workers they represent as unreasonable and themselves as the realists. They seek a softening of struggle, they seek accommodation with owners, and they hate the unrestrained worker self-determination of open-ended strikes. Seeing their unionism not as class struggle but narrowly defined against particular employers, they often believe their role is merely to protect their members from rogue employers, rather than to fight for the entire class. This frequently leads to an exclusionary and often racist unionism that ignores the rest of the working class and sees immigrants and workers around the world as enemies rather than allies.

At the core of business unionism is class collaboration, which means these unionists see their interests more allied with management and owners than with other workers. Rather than seeing bosses as exploitative and our natural enemies, they see the unions as allies of management. This leads business unions to see workers at a plant they represent as being in competition with workers at other plants rather than sharing common interests. Or construction unions fighting for construction jobs to build a Walmart store while ignoring the effect of such an anti-union employer on the rest of the working class. At a broader level, they identify workers from other countries as the problem. For example, in the early 1980s the US auto industry was under competitive pressure from Toyota and other automakers. Even though this was the same time auto management, like other industries, was launching an anti-union offensive, the United Auto Workers chose to attack foreign workers.

For unionists this idea should be simple—labor and management have opposing interests. However, powerful forces in society constantly work to undermine this key principle. Government mediators and university labor educators like to promote what they call win-win bargaining, labor-management cooperation programs, or interest-based bargaining. These concepts all share the view that labor and management share common interests and we just need to figure out how to get to yes.

But we know this cannot be true. On every issue in bargaining, labor and management have opposing interests. When bargaining wages, the billionaires will get a greater share of the wealth that labor produces, or the workers will. In shop floor struggles, workers will work harder and be more exhausted at the end of the shift, or work less. On safety, we want better equipment, and they want to pinch pennies. Labor's gain is management's loss.

Despite this, many union officials support various labor cooperation schemes promoted by management. Sometimes management does this when unions are powerful to lull the unions to sleep. But often they will employ this strategy during periods of relative weakness when they know business unionists will jump at the chance.

For the first couple of decades of the twentieth century, the labor movement was engaged in pitched battles with employers. While many of us have heard of the classic battles of the IWW, the AFL unions also fought for unionization. In certain industries such as streetcars and mining, labor battles looked like armed warfare. Employers relentlessly attacked unions and declared that entire industries would operate on a non-union, open-shop basis.

Yet despite all of this, the leadership of the AFL struck up a partnership with the National Civic Federation (NCF). The NCF was led by industrialist Mark Hanna, with AFL leader Samuel Gompers as vice president. The group preached harmony among classes and labor peace, largely on capital's terms. Although management and labor supposedly came in as equals, Hanna referred to AFL leaders such as Gompers as his lieutenants.[7]

During the 1920s, there were two paths forward for the labor movement. As noted labor historian Philip Foner pointed out, "Convinced they could not win out against the large employers, the AFL leaders pushed the idea that union-management cooperation had to replace labor militancy as the only way to maintain the existence of unions."[8] William Z. Foster explained in his 1927 book *Misleaders of Labor* that class collaboration was deeply rooted in AFL business unionism philosophy: "Between the working class and the capitalist class there rages an inevitable conflict over the division of the products of the workers' labor. . . . The theory of class collaboration denies this basic class struggle. It is built around the false notion of a fundamental harmony of interests between the exploited workers and the exploiting capitalists."[9]

This allowed employers to form alliances with the business union leaders to buy them off.

While Gompers and other AFL officials were being wined and dined, the legendary Mother Jones traveled around wherever workers were struggling. As she testified, "I live in the United States, but I do not know exactly where. My address is wherever there is a fight against oppression."[10] Indeed her autobiography reads of constant struggle and much sorrow. Now, we are not all going to be Mother

Jones, but we can have a similar approach to building struggle.

Likewise, union militants affiliated with the Communist Party waged bitter strikes in southern textile mills, engaged in early auto industry strikes, and built the mining wars of West Virginia and southern Illinois. Although they lost more than they won, these efforts paved the way for the 1930s upsurge.

Later generations of class struggle unionists adopted this approach. During the 1980s and early 1990s, many labor officials fell for labor-management cooperation programs rather than fighting. Unions such as the United Auto Workers and many others worked jointly with management to speed up the pace of work. The group Labor Notes contributed to developing an ideological pole against these jointness programs, publishing books such as *Concessions and How to Beat Them* and several that critique the jointness programs, in which unions partnered with management to operate "more efficiently" so as to better compete with other facilities. In practice this meant the unions got in bed with the company to make workers work harder.

Class struggle unionists coalesced around a different course for the labor movement centered on labor solidarity, strike support, resistance to labor-management cooperation, and worker internationalism. Central to left-wing trade unionism in the 1970s and 1980s was fighting against what these unionists saw as "sellout" union officials. Meatpackers, autoworkers, transit workers, steelworkers, truck drivers, and mineworkers all saw significant reform movements explicitly offering member control and militancy as an alternative path forward for labor.

During the 1980s and 1990s, a vibrant left wing of the labor movement saw militancy as key to reviving labor. In key battles, activists sought to push free from the restrictions in labor law. During the Hormel strike in the mid-1980s, a militant local union sought to break free from the restrictions on solidarity. United Food and Commercial Workers Local P-9 set up picket lines at other plants in the system, argued that fighting concessions was the only way forward for meatpackers, and came into sharp conflict with their national union.

In many other situations, striking local unions who sought to fight back conflicted with their international unions, which favored collaboration. These battles—including paperworkers in Jay, Maine, A.E. Staley workers in the mid-1990s, and *Detroit News* workers— were flashpoints drawing together militant supporters from across the country. The strikes took on an oppositional tone. The Staley workers picketed the 1995 AFL Executive Board meeting, demanding that the AFL leadership back their strikes.

This form of unionism drew sharp lines between workers and employers, engaged in fierce battles, and frequently came into conflict with union leadership. One can tell who the class struggle unionists are by how much they fight the boss and the intensity of the struggle. When the chips are down, and the workers are fighting the boss, do they try to calm things down, or do they join in the struggle and seek to intensify it?

The Working Class Shall Free Itself

Class struggle unionists strongly believe workers should lead their own struggles. When I think of all the class struggle unionists I have known over the years, this quality is the one that stands out. In fact, one can use this as a dividing line feature, helping separate class struggle unionists from other progressive-sounding unionists. Do they believe workers should lead their own movement, or do they think key strategic decisions should be made by staffers far removed from the workplace?

For as long as there has been a socialist movement, there have been middle-class reformers who want to fix things for workers. One of the earliest international workers' groups was the International Workingmen's Association, also called the First International, founded in 1864. It's first point, written by socialist leader Karl Marx, stated "that the emancipation of the working classes must be conquered by the working classes themselves."[11] Of all the possible points to start a manifesto, that may seem like an odd choice. But Marx recognized that there was a long history of different groups in society trying to hijack the workers' movement for their own interests.

Back in the late 1800s when the system of capitalism was young, many middle-class folks such as shop owners and professionals felt squeezed by the new system and sought a dizzying array of solutions. They had a variety of concerns such as currency reform, the gold standard, and more. Some advocated for the greenback, others for land reform, and others for a middle-class socialism. Many sought to divert the labor movement to these causes. Today, many activists are looking at the labor movement in the same way.

It makes sense when you think about it. We have talked about the tremendous power that workers potentially have in the economy and society. As the producers of wealth, workers are the one group in society that has the power to bring the economy to a halt. Middle-class groups traditionally want a piece of that power. Class struggle unionists, however, have insisted on the principle that the working class must lead their own struggles.

Would-be reformers come into the labor movement with all kinds of ideas that may or may not correspond with the ideas of workers. They are correctly driven to unionism by goals of reforming society. But many have not worked in tedious jobs for abusive supervisors week after week. Their versions of unionism invariably lose the shop floor issues and the intensity that worker-led struggles have.

Longtime class struggle unionist Joe Allen explained this fundamental concept well for Democratic Socialists of America labor activists:

> Marxists are guided by one principle in all our work: "The emancipation of the working class must be the work of the working class itself." The international working class today is the most diverse representation of humanity in history, and the only class capable of freeing humanity from the catastrophes that modern capitalism has brought to our species and planet. It is this very democratic and liberatory concept—"self-emancipation"—that distinguishes Marxism from other rival "socialisms" in Marx's time, and has proven a resilient attraction to tens of millions since his death in 1883.[12]

While Allen's quote speaks of socialists, one can also apply it to distinguish class struggle unionists from progressive top-down unionists no matter how left wing they sound.

This belief in worker self-advocacy is a hallmark of class struggle unions. When you look at the historic IWW, the left-led unions of the 1930s to the 1950s, the rank-and-file caucuses of the 1970s, the remaining left-led unions such as the United Electrical Workers and International Longshore and Warehouse Union, the Labor Notes and Teamsters for a Democratic Union trend, and the current IWW, as well as class struggle unionists spread across various unions today, there is one constant variable: a belief in workers.

For every union strategy, every action proposed, we need to ask, where do the workers fit within this strategy? When Occupy activists call for longshore workers to strike, when nonprofits declare publicity strikes that involve few workers, when business unionists settle a contract in the back room, when folks promote a model of unionism reliant on staff organizers and their brilliant techniques, we need to ask, where are the workers?

The Labor Bureaucracy and Class Struggle

Class struggle unionists have long believed that full-time union staffers have different material interests than those of the members. The IWW referred to the AFL staff by various derogatory names such as bureaucrats, labor fakirs, pie cards, and porkchoppers. In the 1930s, class struggle unionists clearly saw differences with the union bureaucracy and sought to chart a different course. For the left-wing groups in the 1970s, the concept of the labor bureaucracy was central to their theory. While the groups vehemently disagreed on how to relate to these officials, few denied the differences. This belief led to a focus on building rank-and-file caucuses, reform movements, and wildcat strikes.

In decades past, union reformers identified it as a problem that there was an entire apparatus called the union bureaucracy. By that they meant that there was an entire apparatus built up within unions of paid staff and elected officials who no longer worked (or never worked, in modern unions like SEIU) in the workplaces they represented. Their full-time existence was spent trying to handle grievances, resolve issues with employers, and administer the affairs of the union. Their material existence, their pay and benefits, working conditions, and station in life differed greatly from the workers they represented.

The incentive to maintain these positions is very great. Everyone in some way is compromised, although few acknowledge or admit it. Union officers have legitimate concerns about the institutions they represent. This constrains their choice of tactics. Union staff and officials, in the back of their minds, know if they are fired they stand to lose pensions and jobs far above what they could command elsewhere. Labor educators rely on the support of unions, and the staff of workers' centers rely on foundation funding for their jobs. Union organizing staff answer to officials higher in the union bureaucracy. All of these careers could be jeopardized by militancy and adopting strategies that confront the union bureaucracy.

Far removed from the oppression of the workplace, these officials are often put in the place of mediating the demands of the workers, and they face the reality of having to compromise with employers within a fundamentally unfair system of labor laws. At its worst, this relationship can lead to a mindset that the officials know more than the unreasonable workers. But even among the most committed, well-intentioned activists, these different realities shape perspectives. You are what you eat, as they say. This is not to say that folks should not become union staff, but understanding the differences between staff positions and working in the workplace is important.

And as in any bureaucracy, there are express and implicit pressures to adhere to group demands. These can be overt, such as the threat of termination for supporting reform movements or militancy. But it can also be pressure to get along by getting contracts settled, not disrupting relationships with employers, and so forth. Even worse: to turn a blind eye to corruption. During the scandal unveiled in 2017 in the United Auto Workers, which included taking gifts from employers, stealing union dues, and shaking down vendors, many participants cited the excuse that they were going along because everyone else did it.

Whether they are conscious of it or not, union staffers are pressured to adopt a philosophy that allows them to keep their jobs. As my cynical law professor used to say, these folks like to do good while doing well for themselves. Nowadays, many of the left wing of labor are concentrated in union staff positions, often in organizing departments of unions, or they work in labor studies programs. Most of the books and articles on labor theory are written by these folks. It should come as no surprise then that much of today's left union theory involves better methods of organizing or adopting progressive positions on social issues. Neither of which challenges the union bureaucracy or jeopardizes staff jobs.

The labor movement today is in miserable shape, probably worse than in any period of labor history. While the labor bureaucracy is not the only cause of labor's weakness, it is a major impediment to union renewal. The United Autoworkers is embroiled in a corruption scandal with a real possibility of federal oversight; most international unions practice business unionism; and the so-called progressive unions such as SEIU are mired in class collaboration, are beset by undemocratic functioning, and are even more staff-driven than more conservative business unions.

Yet much of the labor commentary in recent years in labor-relations journals or progressive labor outlets rarely critiques the union bureaucracy. Instead the focus is on how to organize better or promoting alternative forms of worker organization such as foundation-funded workers' centers. While all of these issues deserve conversation, they obscure both the sad internal shape of the labor movement and the steps necessary to revive our movement.

This does not mean that progressives should not be union staff or that all staff are bad. It does mean that the strategies and approaches staff come up with will not necessarily match the interest of the workers they represent. Class struggle unionists who are in staff positions must be prepared to fight against the pressures to conform, even if it means risking a staff job. It means remembering that the interests and experience you have as a staff member are not the same as the workers working under often oppressive conditions even for unionized employers. This means staff must fight for worker leadership in all decisions.

Previous generations of class struggle unionists promoted rank-and-file control of unions as a central part of their strategies. They put sharp demands upon unions to fight the boss and supported independent efforts of the membership to engage in wildcat strikes and other initiatives not supported by the union hierarchy. Such ideas inevitably came into conflict with trade union officials by promoting intense struggle against the bosses and demanding the labor movement adopt aggressive demands to organize industries.

For this reason, many supported efforts on a local or national level to help the rank and file reform their unions. During the 1970s and beyond, groups such as Miners for Democracy, the Steelworkers Fightback campaign of Ed Sadlowski, and Teamsters for a Democratic Union sought to rid the unions of corruption and put in place class struggle approaches to the crisis of unionism. Class struggle unionists also seek to establish a different relationship between the staff and membership when in the leadership.

Another reason to believe that workers should lead their own movement is quite pragmatic. History shows that worker-led struggle is actually what produces change. In the 1950s, socialist Hal Draper explained that "the conditions and interests of the working class not only push it toward organized struggle against capitalism, but impel it toward *a courage and boldness and militancy* which are well-nigh unique to it, at critical moments of struggle when these qualities are called for."[13]

Think about the wild upsurges of recent decades. In 2012, public employees and supporters rebelled against Wisconsin governor Scott Walker's bill to gut public employee bargaining rights. Thousands of teachers engaged in a grassroots sick-out strike, with thousands occupying the capitol building while tens of thousands of workers marched around the state capital. This effort was driven from below, not from labor strategists or skilled staff organizers.

Likewise, the most significant strikes in recent years have been a set of teacher strikes in Republican-dominated states in the South and Southwest in 2018. Commencing with teachers in West Virginia, teachers in Oklahoma and Arizona engaged in illegal statewide strikes. These actions were rooted in the self-activity of the working class. The actions had both an intensity and a scale of grassroots involvement that eclipsed decades of worker-center and union activity. They were powerful precisely because they were not under the control of the labor establishment.

This belief in workers' self-representation, coupled with the analysis of the labor bureaucracy, lead to a very distinctive brand of unionism that focuses on

- building rank-and-file movements,
- shop floor struggle, and
- fighting for union democracy.

In fact, one can safely say if a "progressive" strain of unionism does not have these features, it is not truly class struggle unionism.

Fight for the Shop Floor

Another way to figure out who is a class struggle unionist is to see how they talk about shop floor struggles. Are their strategies rooted in the workplace? Do workers in the workplace control strategy, or are they merely props for union or nonprofit staffers? Is it all about wages, or do workers' shop floor concerns get dealt with? Invariably, class struggle unionists focus on workplace struggles.

Michael Yates in his book *Can the Working Class Change the World?* explains some of the ways owners can increase their profits: "First, as we have seen, they will rise if the working day is lengthened, other things equal. Similar reasoning tells us profits will fall if the day is shortened. Second, profits will grow if workers labor more intensively during each hour of work, other things being equal (in effect a cut in wages)."[14] By lengthening the workday or making workers labor more intensively, employers change the balance discussed in the previous chapter.

Previously we discussed how a hypothetical employer was able to recoup all of the inputs and the labor in five hours out of an eight-hour shift, in essence pocketing the remaining three hours of labor. But here if the worker works twelve hours, the employer would pocket seven hours' labor rather than merely three. Likewise, if an employer makes the worker work twice as hard, the boss can achieve a similar result. Employers strive to drive down the price of any input, including labor, to the bare minimum, which is the cost of sustaining the labor force.

For this reason, fights over the length of the workday and the control of the shop floor have been at the heart of trade union struggle. Many middle-class supporters of labor ignore this reality and often focus simply on wages. But while wages matter, most employers understand that making workers work harder is often a better way of increasing corporation profits. Employers focus on what they see as productivity. This is a key area of class struggle and a key element in virtually every strike in recent decades. The reason is simple—we can fight whether employers give a 3 or 5 percent raise, but if they can make us work ten times harder, they win every time.

But equally important, the shop floor struggle is key to defending human dignity. Employers seek to treat human labor like any other commodity that is an input into production. As legal scholar James Pope points out, it is not possible to separate the labor employers seek from the workers who supply it. So while management buys a worker's ability to work for their shift, the worker is a human being who wants to be free. Work is tied up with personhood, and it is hard to be free when you are abused for eight or more hours each day at work. This creates a natural conflict.

When an employer hires a worker, they are hiring the worker's capacity to produce labor over a period of time. As economics professor Richard Hyman explains,

> If labour within capitalism is in one sense a commodity like any other, in another sense it is unlike all other types of commodity. For while the employment contract may well specify precisely what the worker receives from the employer, what he/she provides in return is rarely defined specifically. The worker does not

agree to sell an exact quantity of labour; for neither physical nor intellectual work can normally be quantified precisely. . . . Rather than agreeing to expend a given amount of effort, the employee surrenders his/her *capacity to work*; and it is the function of management, through its hierarchy of control, to transform this capacity into actual productive activity.[15]

This makes the shop floor struggle a key component of class struggle. Historically many of the great strikes have generated from shop floor issues. In classic labor history books such as *Workers' Control in America* and *The Fall of the House of Labor*, labor historian David Montgomery detailed how the employer's drive to take over production stoked massive resistance in the early 1900s, when skilled production workers resisted management's efforts to deskill their work.[16] Micah Uetricht and Barry Eidlin, in their systematic review of left-wing union strategy, note how class struggle unionists focused on shop floor power, concluding that "radicals' beliefs in the illegitimacy of management's authority on the shop floor led to their refusal to cede control of shop-floor conditions to management. This differed from liberal unionists who believed unions should fight for better pay and benefits, but that decisions about the pace and nature of work were management's prerogative."[17]

These issues are direct and immediate for the workers involved. For teachers it's how many students in the classroom; for drywallers it's how many boards a day; for autoworkers it's how many seconds per minute you can catch your breath; for nurses it's the ratio of nurses to patients. But beyond staffing, what is the control and autonomy on the shop floor or the workplace? What is the pace of work? Who controls the workplace? Are supervisors put in their place? What is it like going to work each day?

An employer who wants to pocket more money tries to force workers to work harder and longer in a workday. In most unionized industries, this comes down to who controls the shop floor and the workplace.

Kim Moody has written extensively about management's drive to intensify work. In his book *On New Terrain* he discusses how a large part of the reduction in manufacturing jobs has been achieved by making workers work longer, harder, and with fewer breaks. Moody concludes,

> All of these changes taken together have led to one of the biggest job-destroying intensifications of labor in the history of capitalism. By the second decade of the twenty-first century, if you survived the process, your job had been stressed, reengineered, measured, monitored, standardized, intensified, and connected just in time to another stressed, reengineered, etc., job while you and your fellow workers had been informed that you were the organization's most valuable asset. After all, who could produce so much surplus value so fast at virtually no extra cost?[18]

Management has long understood, far better than many labor analysts, the importance of undercutting work rules in union contracts. As one who has bargained union contracts for thirty years, I know from experience this is where the real money is, not in fighting over a 3 percent wage increase. It's why a good proportion of the life-and-death strikes of recent decades have been over work rules.

Coming out of the upsurge of the 1930s, workers ruled the shop floor in many industries. If they did not like what a supervisor did, they would stop work until the problem was resolved. These ministrikes gave workers an incredible amount of control at the point of production. They also infuriated management representatives who sought to regain control.

Many labor officials were uncomfortable with worker militancy and prized their relationships with corporate leaders. They sought to get the situation under control and stop unauthorized strikes. During the 1940s and 1950s, as unions became more institutionalized, management pressured unions to control the workers and to obey now, grieve later.

The landmark 1950 United Auto Workers agreement, negotiated by Walter Reuther, explicitly adopted a framework that gave workers productivity increases in exchange for giving up the struggle to control the shop floor, agreeing to management's rights, a five-year contract, and accepted the framework, which meant the company received all the profits. The five-year contract, known as the Treaty of Detroit, was hailed by *Fortune* magazine as abandoning class struggle principles: "It is the first major union contract that explicitly accepts objective economic facts—cost of living and productivity—as determining wages, thus throwing overboard all theories of wages as determined by political power and of profit as 'surplus value.'"[19]

Under this framework, shop floor militancy needed to be tamed.

In her book *The Long Deep Grudge*, labor historian Toni Gilpin explains how the approach of the left-led Farm Equipment Workers (FE) union representing workers at International Harvester differed from that of the UAW. Unlike the UAW, the FE union fought the notion of limited productivity increases. Between 1945 and 1954, the union engaged in over one thousand strikes at International Harvester plants, filed thousands of grievances, and fought the company on every turn.[20] Even though they had bargaining agreements, class war continued during the term of the agreement.

A typical shop floor dispute might begin when a supervisor threatens a worker or denies a preferential pay rate. As FE shop floor leader Jim Mouser explained, when he would approach a supervisor over an issue of speeding up the work or another dispute, he would tell the supervisor he had the entire group behind him: "Well, I'll tell you right now. It's not just him, it's the whole department. When that bell sounds at 7:30 and they go on their break, they're going to have a meeting. If you haven't straightened it out, you won't have any pieces from anybody the rest of the night, because they're going to go home. They've already told me that."[21]

If the supervisor did not relent, the workers would shut down the factory or plant.

Management understood the need to control the workplace. Reuther's UAW teamed up with the anti-union International Harvester management to fight the FE at every turn. They relentlessly raided the FE with management's full support. Eventually by the mid-1960s, the FE was no more, absorbed into the UAW. Other class struggle unions such as the United Electrical Workers union and the tobacco workers were similarly attacked.

Underlying the attack on class struggle unions was a fight for control of the workplace. As Andrew Kolin indicates, "Behind the Red Scares lurked the fear of labor that wasn't under the complete domination of capital."[22] The major offensives against labor have occurred when employers want to restructure the workplace, from Fordist production in the 1920s to lean auto production of the 1980s, and were motivated by management's desire to institute control over the workplace. As Kolin puts it, "The ultimate aim then, in using labor repression inside the workplaces, amounts to dividing and conquering any semblance of working class political consciousness at work"[23]

In the book *Left Out,* Judith Stepan-Norris and Maurice Zeitlin examine in detail contracts from left-led CIO unions versus their AFL counterparts. The authors look at contract provisions such as management rights clauses, the right to strike during the contract, length of contract, and the like. They concluded that "the contracts won by locals of the Communist-led internationals were far more likely than those run by their rivals to be prolabor or to counter capital's hegemony in the sphere of production."[24] Class struggle unionism offered a different path to fighting capital flight and deunionization.

In many industries in the 1950s and 1960s, strong unions won and enforced local practices that allowed workers to leave when a set amount of work was done. For some this meant going in the breakroom and playing cards, for some it meant coming back and clocking in at the end of a shift, and for others it meant simply going home. It took strong local unions to enforce these agreements.

In the early 1970s, in the face of falling profits, management launched an offensive to take back control of the shop floor, leading to one of the great wildcat strike waves in US history. At Chrysler in the late 1960s, for example, notes labor writer A. C. Jones, "the number of grievances exploded upward, as company demands increased, tension on the shop floor rose, and union leaders assumed ever greater responsibility for enforcing order on the shop floor."

Wildcat strikes rose dramatically at Chrysler from fifteen in the early 1960s to sixty-seven in the early 1970s.[25]

When Chrysler wanted to ramp up production in light of record sales, since "no new labor-saving plant or equipment had been introduced, the only way the company could increase production to meet demand was to intensify labor, lengthen the working day, ignore the impact on the health and safety of the workers. It was a recipe for resistance."[26]

In the early 1970s, workers engaged in a great strike wave, mainly wildcat strikes in opposition to both their union leadership and the companies. But the business unions largely surrendered control of the workplace. Tom Laney is a retired autoworker at the Ford plant in Saint Paul, Minnesota, and a former union officer long involved in attempting to reform the UAW and put the union on a class struggle basis. Laney forged ties with Mexican autoworkers over the objections of the UAW national leadership and fought the jointness programs throughout the 1980s. Laney was asked when he thought the UAW adopted the corporate model: "They refused to take up the speedup fight in the mid-70s. To me, real unions fight the speedup—or they're not a union. When the district committeemen started selling bogus time standards, the real UAW was gone."[27]

The UAW was not alone in this as many unions abandoned the flight for the shop floor.

Today's unionism has largely abandoned the fight for control of the workplace. As legal scholar James Atleson notes, after detailing the ways in which management dominates even unionized shops, "Collective bargaining has no relationship with the modern conception of industrial democracy for it accepts as a basic premise the authoritarian and bureaucratic nature of the enterprise."[28]

It is hard to envision class struggle unionism not rooted in the workplace. The workplace is where value is created by, and stolen from, workers; the place where workers come together across race, gender, and nationality; and the location where ordinary people can directly bring society to a halt. Initiatives that are not rooted in the workplace and among workers are more akin to social work than class struggle.

Class Stand

Class struggle unionists see our unionism as part of a larger struggle between labor and capital. This leads to a more critical analysis of the role of the media, government, the courts, and the main political parties, including the Democratic Party. It leads to an antiestablishment brand of unionism that approaches all questions from the standpoint of class struggle.

Underlying the billionaire class's great fortunes is a whole set of institutions in society that are geared toward defending power and privilege. As Michael Parenti noted in his classic book *Democracy for the Few,* "Those who control the wealth of society, the corporate plutocracy, exercise trusteeship over educational institutions, foundations, think tanks, publications, and mass media, thereby greatly influencing society's ideological output and information flow. They also wield a power over political life far in excess of their number."[29]

Billionaires own the media and fund the foundations, and political spending by the superrich and corporate interests dwarfs what unions can provide.

Previously, we discussed how the economic system allows employers to take billions of dollars of the wealth produced by working people. This wealth in the form of capital is used in turn to produce greater and greater fortunes. But what is wealth? It is not something you can hold in your hand. It is a social relationship—the ability to command others. It is power. Politically, this wealth has often been used to buy politicians and control the political system.

An even bigger problem is that the entire political and economic system is built to provide for the exploitation of workers by the billionaire class. Previously we discussed that the billionaire class has power because they control the income-producing wealth of society. Underpinning the employers' power is a system that gives certain people the rights to the proceeds of labor because they are the owners of industry.

But where does this ownership and control come from? It is not something that exists in nature. (The defenders of the billionaire class like to talk as if this control is the natural order of things.) In fact, the idea that three people should own more than 250 million people is quite nonsensical and unnatural.

In the 1960s, British writer E. P. Thompson wrote *The Making of the English Working Class*, a magnificent book that details how the emerging system of capitalism pushed peasants off the land from the 1600s to the 1800s, destroying common areas and replacing them with private property. Workers were driven from the land and communities into teaming industrial hellholes where they had to work in miserable conditions in order to survive.

For this reason, the early trade union struggles were very explosive affairs, a combination of strikes and riots or uprisings. The great railroad strike of 1877 was an explosion of the community against the giant railroads that were dominating the economy and disrupting the old way of life. The working class buckled against the imposition of this unnatural and unequal system.

If the idea that a handful of people can control the product of many does not exist in nature, where does it come from? The answer is very important for union strategy. Private ownership of income-producing wealth stems from the control of one class of people over another. The entire framework of the government and the courts is to protect this system. It is why the government will never be truly neutral in labor disputes.

For these reasons, class struggle unionists have consistently been willing to violate labor law over the decades. From the IWW defiance of free speech rights in the early 1900s to the mass picketing and sit-down strikes of the 1930s, from millions of public employees illegally striking in the 1960s to the wildcat strikes of the 1970s and the promotion of militancy of the 1980s, class struggle unionists have a long, proud history of rejecting the status quo.

Class struggle unionists are deeply suspicious of the role of the government in protecting workers' rights. Our unionism does not consider government institutions such as the National Labor Relations Board and the federal courts to be neutral institutions. Rather, anti-unionism is built into the role of the government as the protector

of the billionaire ownership and control of the income-producing seg-
ments of society. This fundamental understanding leads to an entirely
different approach to unionism and politics.

But seeing unionism as part of a larger class struggle highlights
the need for a strategic approach. Our unionism is about contend-
ing with capital on a national scale, rather than simply a question of
organizing workers. That requires an understanding of key industries and strategic approaches that will be the subject of discussion
in chapter 7.

Chapter 3

Beyond Labor Liberalism

To revive class struggle unionism, we need to break with a distinct form of unionism that I call *labor liberalism*. For the last several decades, labor liberalism has been the dominant trend within the labor movement. Because many progressive unionists are influenced by this tendency, this may be an uncomfortable discussion.

Most of the AFL-CIO unions were very bureaucratic and ineffective in the 1980s. The AFL-CIO promoted anti-immigrant policies and worked with the Central Intelligence Agency to undermine worker movements around the world. AFL-CIO officials were extremely hostile to socialist groups and distrustful of progressive social movements. Many international unions actively undermined strikes by militant local unions during this period in the 1980s and were completely unprepared for management's union-busting onslaught.

Labor liberalism emerged as a third way, situated between the confrontational rank-and-file approach of the class struggle unionists and the conservative business unionists. Leading the charge was a grouping of 1960s social movement activists who turned to the labor movement to transform society. By the mid-1980s many had drifted into graduate school, but some who remained had risen to the midlevel of the labor movement, including staff jobs in the organizing and education departments of unions. With the labor movement reeling from a vicious deunionization effort, space opened for a more progressive form of unionism.

Adherents of the approach gained influence in many international unions, particularly the SEIU. The SEIU in the 1990s was aggressively self-confident, with their purple shirts proclaiming they were "Leading the Way." During this period, they advocated for organizing the unorganized, a protest movement approach, and progressive positions on social issues. The overall program was characterized as the organizing approach.

Running with the New Voice slate, SEIU president John Sweeney launched a contested election for president of the AFL-CIO, defeating business unionist Thomas R. Donahue in 1995. The New Voice slate promised to repair ties with the academic left, to organize the unorganized, and to form alliances with liberal political groups.

In the realm of tactics, they favored moving away from the bitter defensive, open-ended strikes of the 1980s toward utilizing corporate campaigns, one-day strikes, and other staff-controlled methods of class struggle. These tactics were billed as fighting smarter. But they also pushed for a restructuring of unions in a top-down fashion in order to shift more resources into organizing, an approach sharply at odds with the class struggle union approach.

Labor Liberalism Defined

So what is labor liberalism and why should it be considered a distinct union philosophy? Labor liberalism is a form of unionism that straddles the fence between business unionism and class struggle unionism. Labor liberals adopt the progressive political views of the middle-class social movements but reject the traditional workplace organization and concerns of both traditional unionism and class struggle unionism.

Whereas traditional business unionism focuses on immediate needs of workers, concentrating on things such as work rules and unjust discipline, labor liberals look outward for what they believe are solutions to workers' problems, including fighting to raise the minimum wage and protective legislation. Labor liberalism centers its gravity outside the workplace, using unionism to influence politicians to win improvements for groups of workers, whereby unions become a mixture of social advocacy group and pressure group on the Democratic Party.

While traditional unionism, even bureaucratic business unionism, had its starting point in workplaces, labor liberalism is centered in nonprofits, in academia, and among the staff of unions, particularly ones without much rank-and-file control over decision-making. Traditional unionism grew from the ground up, starting in particular workplaces and labor markets.

The main practitioners of this labor-liberalism form of unionism include the SEIU, certain initiatives such as the Fight for $15, much of the worker-center movement, and some but not all advocates of social movement unionism. But their ideas have extended far beyond this core group, providing the basis for much labor commentary and providing the framework for discussion at the national AFL-CIO. Many of the initiatives of the last decades such as alternative unionism and sectoral bargaining spring from this set of ideas.

I propose using the term *labor liberalism* for a number of reasons. First, it stands in a middle or liberal position between the radicalism of class struggle unionism and the conservatism of business unionism. Second, labor liberalism's strategy is geared toward getting Democrats to pass protective labor legislation, such as increasing the minimum wage. It has more in common with nonprofits rooted in the middle class than it does with worker-led unionism. Finally, because labor liberalism strategy does not challenge capital, but like business unionism accepts the existing system, it fits better within the existing tradition of liberalism rather than more radical socialist and other anticapitalist traditions.

Some could argue that, since labor liberalism does not break with business unionism, it could simply be labeled a variety of business unionism. There is merit to this position, as there has always been a moderate socialist or progressive wing within business unionism that advocates more progressive positions than the main reactionary wing of the labor movement. In the 1920s, William Z.

Foster wrote in *Misleaders of Labor* that, in addition to the corrupt business union trend, there also existed progressive and socialist trends within the labor movement but that these often gave progressive cover to the do-nothing AFL leadership of the time.

In the 1930s and beyond, a wing of the labor movement typified by Sidney Hillman of Amalgamated Clothing Workers of America favored close identification with the New Deal wing of the Democratic Party. Later, anticommunist leaders such as Walter Reuther of the UAW combined progressive policy positions with a purging of class struggle unionism and destruction of shop floor organization. So this idea that one could combine liberal positions on social issues with a rejection of class floor shop struggle has a long history in the labor movement.

But here, the labor liberals do not merely append progressive positions onto business unionism; they reject many fundamentals of trade union theory. On key questions such as workplace-based organization, jurisdiction, bargaining, and strike theory, labor liberalism deviates significantly from traditional union theory. In fact, while labor liberalism is more progressive than business unionism on many sociopolitical questions, on questions of worker representation and struggle with employers, it is often more conservative.

The chart below highlights the main features of the various forms of unionism. Many unions will have elements of two or all three forms. It's also important to note that even though labor liberalism has represented the main ideological trend for the last two decades, huge swaths of the labor movement have never really fallen under its spell. The building trades represent a large plurality of the labor movement, and many industrial unions never truly went with it. Others dabbled in it at the international level while the day-to-day of their locals adhered to business unionism.

	Business Unionism	Labor Liberalism	Class Struggle Unionism
Examples	Many AFL-CIO unions from 1950s–1980s, current building trades, UAW, and many local unions and some international unions	SEIU, most workers' centers, many central labor councils	Current UE, historic IWW, International Longshore and Warehouse Union, Chicago Teachers Union, and left-led unions of the 1930s and beyond
Shop Floor Organization	Some form of shop floor organization, although bureaucratic in nature	Mostly abandons the shop floor; centers unionism far away from the workplace	Core belief in shop floor organization
Union Democracy	As unions, have elections of officers and procedures for strike votes, etc.; bureaucracy valued more than democracy	Low priority, often more undemocratic than business unions; workers' centers often lack formal democratic mechanisms of unions	Core belief in union democracy
Role of Middle Class	Path to the top often through the ranks; heavy reliance on professional staff	Leading theorists and other leaders are middle class; expunges distinctions between middle class activists and leaders	Core belief in working class self-liberation

Organizing the Unorganized	Low priority	Top priority in the 1990s even at the expense of representing current members; now often focused on raising standards through government action	High priority but not at the expense of enforcing existing agreements
Positions on Social Issues	Often centrist or conservative	Progressive	Very progressive / left wing
Conflict with Employers	Downplayed although could flare up; often favors labor-management cooperation	Will use confrontational tactics to organize but then collaborate with employers	High priority

The Difficulties in Critiquing Labor Liberalism

Some of the most difficult conversations are among friends. Arguing with our enemies is easy, but for those who have worked within unions and other social organizations, we know that dealing with contradictions among the people is one of the most difficult but important things we do. This is especially true when it comes to the critique of labor liberalism.

The labor liberals for decades have occupied the commanding heights of labor theory. Labor liberals hold important positions in many unions, among the labor press, and as labor educators. And frankly, they write a lot—way more than most worker-activists do. Even more important, many of their ideas make sense: of course we need to organize the unorganized, have broad bargaining demands, and take progressive stances on political issues. Because labor liberalism comes out of the left/liberal social movement, they naturally adopt the language of those movements.

And frankly, those who advocate a class struggle approach have not been very good about offering an alternative that makes sense. This is largely due to the lack of an anticapitalist movement in this country. Since the early 1980s, the left in this country has been weak and on the defensive. The labor movement suffered catastrophic setbacks in the 1980s, and other social movements fared little better. Since the 1980s, conservative ideas have ruled, and until recently, socialist ideas were marginalized.

Quite naturally, those who want a better labor movement have gravitated to labor liberal ideas. After all, they offer a seeming alternative to business unionism. The existing labor movement has been bureaucratic and conservative and does not seem to offer much for working people. So, much good work has been done under the banner of labor liberalism.

But times are changing. In the last decade we have seen the Occupy movement, the Wisconsin uprising, the red state teacher revolts, the strike wave of the Chicago teachers and others, and the rise of democratic socialist politicians such as Bernie Sanders and Alexandria Ocasio-Cortez. Many younger folks gravitating to the labor movement are looking for radical ideas. The basis is here for a new type of labor movement. We have the opportunity to move beyond labor liberalism.

One of my favorite organizers in the labor movement, Ellen David Friedman, told me she likes to talk about theory with new activists, explaining they have a choice to pick which framework they want to adopt. It's time to choose a new framework that goes beyond labor liberalism. It has served its purpose, but we cannot move forward under its banner.

The problem with labor liberalism is not necessarily what it includes but what it does not include. Labor liberalism talks about progressive social issues and a broad approach of representing the working class. But it leaves out many aspects of class struggle unionism such as sharp class-on-class struggle, the fight for the shop floor, union reform, and other elements. After decades of experimenting, it is clear labor liberalism is not up to the challenge that faces us. We need class struggle unionism.

Labor Liberalism versus Class Struggle Unionism

The AFL-CIO during the 1980s was staunchly anticommunist and hostile to traditional class struggle ideas. Those who are newer to the labor movement may be used to a certain openness to left-wing or socialist ideas nowadays, especially with the popularity of politicians such as Sanders and Ocasio-Cortez. But that was not always the case. From the 1950s to the 1980s, there was very little space for open leftists.

When I entered the labor movement in the mid-1980s, the movement was fiercely anticommunist and hostile to outsiders. When I first ran for statewide union office, one of the officers sat me down and said, some folks are saying you're pink. It took me a bit to realize he was saying I was a socialist. But that was the state of things back then.

Perhaps for that reason, labor liberalism arose as a challenge to business unionism within a very limited framework. As Bill Fletcher and Fernando Gapasin note in *Solidarity Divided*, "Rather than use potentially inflammatory terms like *class struggle unionism*—and to influence the tactics of liberal-to-progressive labor leaders—the proponents of the organizing model suggested the existing movement take significant, though limited, steps to promote real change."[1] While this allowed labor liberals to gain influence in labor, it did not provide the basis for a decisive break with business unionism.

In retrospect, labor liberalism was not as much of a break from business unionism as promised. Class struggle unionists value rank-and-file self-liberation, grassroots militancy, and challenges to the labor bureaucracy. But labor liberalism offered instead tightly choreographed workers' struggles, a dominant role for staff organizers, and an orientation toward passing protective labor legislation.

Labor liberalism required a vilification of traditional unionism from a left/liberal perspective. As labor scholar Stephanie Ross notes, "Social unionism's consistently positive comparison with 'stale' business unionism rests on an idealization of the former, and an overly stark and not-quite accurate dichotomization of the two approaches."[2] In doing so, labor liberalism redefined business unionism, which historically meant unionism that did not challenge the capitalist system.

Instead the concept of business unionism popularized in the 1980s went after only a narrow group—the racist, exclusionary right wing of labor typified by the building trades and the AFL leadership of the time. Although labor liberalism sharply critiques business unionism, the assault has been situated in middle-class progressive theory, with the critique more focused on the exclusionary nature of the AFL and their failure to organize the unorganized. A class struggle perspective would have required an attack on the labor bureaucracy and class collaborationism. Although labor liberals have critiqued right-wing business unionists, it has not been all-out warfare.

In contrast, class struggle unionism and business unionism are mutually exclusive worldviews. While in times of great struggle with employers these viewpoints can coexist temporarily, eventually the two worldviews come into conflict. In the 1910s the IWW was hated by the AFL, which scabbed on IWW strikes. During the 1920s, Communist Party activists were expelled and repressed by the AFL. In the 1930s, although the CIO opened up to the left, this alliance was short-lived and filled with conflict. The AFL and CIO soon declared war on class struggle unionists as part of the red-baiting of the 1940s and 1950s. Class struggle unionism and business unionism are inherently antagonistic.

In contrast, labor liberalism has peacefully coexisted with business unionism for almost thirty years. The reason is simple: labor liberalism does not challenge business unionism.

- Politically, labor liberalism lines up with the progressive wing of the Democratic Party.
- On strike strategy, labor liberalism favors controlled actions that don't risk injunctions that threaten union treasuries.
- Labor liberalism does not embrace militancy or sharp class-on-class struggle that causes ruptures with the employing class.
- In structure, labor liberalism is a top-down version of

unionism, perhaps even more so than traditional business unionism.

- The main themes of labor liberalism are compatible with holding union staff jobs.
- Labor liberalism does not challenge business unionism's fundamental accommodation with capitalism.

Labor liberalism attempts to straddle between two world-views—class struggle unionism and business unionism. And like many attempts at compromise, it fails. So, the question we must ask is, if labor liberalism is such a challenge to the labor establishment, why has it generated such little conflict?

Labor Liberalism Compared with Class Struggle Unionism

Many adherents of labor liberalism would likely say they are practicing left-wing unionism. After all, they adopt the language of middle-class social movements. But labor liberalism bears little resemblance to historical class struggle unionism. So one way to examine the philosophy is to look at how labor liberalism compares to the main features of class struggle unionism. If labor liberalism doesn't match class struggle unionism, it's not it.

Sharp Class Struggle

In the previous chapter we discussed that a hallmark of class struggle unionism is intense class-on-class struggle. But labor liberals hate, fear, and avoid sharp class-on-class struggle, perhaps even more so than business unionists do. Now, this can be hard to see sometimes because labor liberals love action, bold plans, and even taking on bosses. They hold rallies, conduct short strikes, wage campaigns such as the Fight for $15, and propose bold initiatives. On the surface it appears they are militant.

But their actions are carefully controlled affairs: the short-duration strikes, the public relations strikes, and the corporate campaigns. These tactics put pressure on management but in a way that does not allow things to spiral out of labor liberals' control. Typically, a business unionist hesitates to call a strike because no one knows when it will end. Not so with one-day strikes. We all know how that will end—twenty-four hours later!

Traditionally, strikes have been the great equalizer of power within unions and a key mechanism for class struggle unionists to push class struggle and expand their influence. This is important because, even in bureaucratic unions, strikes opened the door to transformative experiences and rank-and-file power. But labor liberals have taken the strike away from the rank and file.

This is particularly true of publicity strikes, which include a small handful of fast-food workers with a large contingent of union staff or supporters. As some organizers quipped, at these publicity strikes there are twenty paid staff and a handful of fired fast-food workers. My point is not to trash this work but to point out that it fundamentally differs from the intense open-ended strikes favored by class struggle unionists historically (and indeed by most business unionists).

Now, the labor liberal strategist would say they are protecting workers and preventing them from getting fired with carefully devised strategies. But for the traditional labor movement, that is why we have strike votes and strike authorization procedures. These are treated as serious affairs, but it is up to the workers to decide.

What would have happened with the labor liberals in charge of the great battles of labor history? The great New York garment workers' strike of 1909 kicked off when a young immigrant, Clara Lemlich, made an impassioned speech. After listening to a speaker go on and on at Cooper Union college, Lemlich demanded action: "I have listened to all the speakers, and I have no further patience for talk. I am a working girl, one of those striking against intolerable conditions. I am tired of listening to speakers who talk in generalities. What we are here for is to decide whether or not to strike. I make a motion that we go out in a general strike."[3]

Now Lemlich would not have been allowed to make such a speech with a worker center or labor liberal union. Workers are typically used as props by the labor liberals, trotted out to give scripted remarks.

To revive the labor movement in the private sector will require violating labor law and sharp confrontation with the existing order. Labor liberalism is incapable of accomplishing this both because of its weak philosophy but also because the leadership is compromised by their positions within the establishment (labor staff, law professors, nonprofit staff). For both ideological and practical reasons, the liberation of the working class will require working-class leadership.

Because labor liberals have adopted the language and demands of progressive social movements, it has been hard for many people to see that abandonment of sharp class conflict was central to labor liberalism's project. But despite the progressive rhetoric and media events, many leaders hold a soft view on management. In the 1990s, under Andy Stern, the Service Employees International Union claimed to offer a different path forward for labor. SEIU was a key player in electing John Sweeney and the New Voice leadership, which promised to rebuild ties with left social movements. But the core of their project was not class struggle.

Many in the labor movement were disgusted in 2019 but not surprised when Stern joined the board of directors of a union-busting group that promotes charter schools. Even though Stern claimed to be leading the way for the labor movement in the 1990s, his union philosophy was one of labor–management collaboration. Rather than seeing that his job was to fight the company, Stern spoke of how he could "build relationships with employers that added value to their businesses as well as to our workers' paychecks."[4]

Stern set up joint committees at the health-care provider Kaiser and gushed, "I attended an early negotiating session in which each issue committee reported on their progress. Listening to the workers and management speaking was an amazing experience: As hard as I tried, I could not distinguish the union representatives from the management representatives."[5] To Stern, that was a good thing, although most union members would like their representatives to sound different from company officials.

Since 2018 former Seattle SEIU leader David Rolf has been peddling a particularly noxious brand of labor capitalism. Teaming up with liberal venture capitalists, Rolf set up a "worker laboratory" that sought to promote worker entrepreneurship by giving out $150,000 grants. Rather than supporting militants or rank-and-file control, the grant givers predictably favored initiatives such as creating new cell phone apps, cooperating with employers to set labor standards, and providing services.[6]

So are these examples aberrations, or are they central to the project? Labor writer Steve Early has spent years chronicling the problems with the SEIU form of unionism, including in his 2011 book *The Civil Wars in US Labor*. Early zeros in on many faults with the SEIU model, including the abandonment of workplace struggle, the leading role of Harvard-educated staff, the disdain for union democracy, and the use of 1-800 numbers for processing grievances rather than a shop steward system. Early makes clear that the outcome of this philosophy is a type of unionism divorced from the workers.

Ultimately, labor liberals need to be judged by the same standards as we judge business unionism. When labor liberal unions propose partnership with employers, when Restaurant Opportunities Centers United proposes a model employer framework, they are not engaged in class struggle unionism. It is class collaboration.

Working-Class Control

In chapter 2 we discussed that a hallmark of class struggle unionism is the belief that workers need to emancipate themselves. But the core of labor liberalism is that the staff of unions and workers' centers lead the workers' movement. This represents a key difference from class struggle unionism. Labor liberals seek to save workers; class struggle unionists seek to help workers liberate themselves.

One way that nonworkers assume control of the workers' movement is to pretend that class differences don't exist. Many progressive activists work as staff for unions or workers' centers or for progressive groups advocating for workers' rights. That's all good work. The problem begins when, instead of seeing themselves as assisting the workers' movement, they see themselves as *the* leaders of the workers' movement. This is particularly true of labor liberal unions such as the SEIU where staff don't need to work their way up from the workplace.

But the idea that you can be a unionist without roots in the labor movement is a recent development. For previous generations of middle-class leftists, going into the labor movement was crossing the class line. In the 1920s, Powers Hapgood was a Harvard graduate who attached himself to workers' struggles. His entering the labor movement was a journey to a different class. Hapgood fought for the miners' reform movement and later joined up with the CIO under John Lewis.

To unionists of his time, Hapgood's class background made him stand out. During a contentious debate in 1923 between John Lewis and mineworker and union reformer John Brophy, Lewis attacked Hapgood for being from the middle class. But "Brophy vigorously defended Hapgood: 'It is true that he has the misfortune of being a college graduate. . . . [Yet] guns have been shoved up against this body. He has been imprisoned. He has gone through the test of whether or not his conduct has been that of a man and a union man.'"[7]

Following in Hapgood's footsteps, Len De Caux was an upper-class British college graduate who wanted to cross the class line and join the labor movement. Calculating this would be hard to do in England with its more rigid class lines, De Caux came to the United States. A friend suggested, "I do like Powers Hapgood, a Harvard man who'd wanted to become integrated in the labor movement. Young, strong, adventurous, Hapgood broke away by 'bumming around the country.' Going from one labor job to another, he ended up as a coal miner."[8] De Caux did just that, riding the rails, working in labor camps, and joining the labor movement.

The point is not that these two men should not have joined the labor movement. Both made valuable contributions over a period of decades. Hapgood was part of the mineworkers' reform movement of the 1920s and later went on to help organize with the CIO. De

Caux was a Wobbly and later one of the highest-placed communists in the CIO as communications director. But it was acknowledged that they were crossing class lines and that class differences exist.

Likewise, many middle-class leftists who entered the labor movement in the 1970s very clearly saw themselves entering another class. According to writer and activist Max Elbaum, part of the labor experience for the 1970s leftists turned worker-activists was integrating with the working class:

> The centerpiece was ensuring that the majority of cadre (from whatever class, racial or educational background) shared the material conditions of working class life. This translated into most living in poorer neighborhoods and getting blue collar jobs—including the most exhausting, dangerous and low-paying. Others sought clerical or secretarial work in large offices, or employment as nurse's aides, nurses or clerks in hospitals and nursing homes.[9]

Fitting in meant learning the customs and outlook of the workers.

On a lighter note, liberal labor lawyer Thomas Geoghegan in his popular 1990s book *Which Side Are You On?* joked about sneaking away to Chicago's liberal enclave Hyde Park from the gritty steel mills neighborhood of South Chicago. "When I first saw Hyde Park, I felt like a sailor seeing land . . . the brick town houses, the bookstores, the BMWs on the street."[10] Geoghegan was a college-educated activist helping out on Ed Sadlowski's 1977 campaign for United Steelworkers of America president and was clearly an outsider in the rough area of South Chicago. While Geoghegan was poking fun at himself and his cohorts, he was recognizing that class differences exist and that he was joining a different class.

Labor liberalism, however, simply ignores that a class divide exists. Andy Stern, who was the leader of labor liberalism as the head of the SEIU in the 1990s, explained, "I was born to white-collar, professional parents in a community where unions were rarely mentioned. . . . I went to an Ivy League college and never held a union job until I started working as a social service worker in 1972."[11] Once in office, Stern "installed a 'new class' of local union managers, drawn from his college-educated staff, who were personally loyal to him and lacked workplace roots (and sometimes even union experience.)"[12]

The Service Employees International Union demolished the smaller locals and placed workers into mega-locals embracing entire regions of the country, making it virtually impossible for workers to reform their unions. Steve Early noted, "I became increasingly concerned that some progressive unionists were not only abandoning 'participatory democracy,' a still-worthwhile sixties notion, they were also creating union structures which would disenfranchise workers to a greater degree than 'old guard' unions do."[13]

Whereas class struggle unionists were known for their commitment to union democracy, the labor liberals became known for their arrogant disregard for workers' self-representation. SEIU is an extreme example, but other institutions of labor liberalism have similar structures. Workers' centers, which will be discussed in detail later in chapter 6, are often initiated by activists from outside the communities they claim to represent, and although they may involve worker-activists, they lack the formal democracy inherent in unions.

The concept that workers should lead their own movement should be familiar to activists who come from other social movements where it is well accepted that the oppressed group should provide leadership and other folks should relate as allies. Decades after the civil rights movement rebelled against the dominant role of white activists within the early civil rights organizations, many in labor still think it is acceptable for middle-class activists to assume leadership of the workers' movement. Folks who come from left social movements who would never dream of poaching in another group's experience have zero problem claiming the identity of a unionist despite no history of having held working-class jobs.

The Shop Floor

The third principle of class struggle unionism is a belief in building struggle in the workplace. Again, labor liberals are probably less similar to class struggle unionism than business unionism is. Labor liberalism situates union efforts far from the worksites involved, which should be a problem for anyone who wants a militant workers' movement. For example, much of the Fight for $15 effort has involved a media air war utilizing publicity strikes involving few workers, rather than an approach of building shop floor committees and fighting fast-food management store by store.

In the 1990s, the SEIU promoted an organizing approach that said in order to raise union density, it is necessary to restructure unions to put resources into organizing rather than representing existing members. Workplace grievances were downplayed in favor of broader objectives. The traditional shop steward approach involved stewards going toe-to-toe with supervisors to defend union members from discipline. But in the SEIU organizing approach, individual grievances were deemed unimportant. In some locals, shop stewards were replaced with a 1-800 number where folks who had no direct experience would handle the grievances.[14] The result was a form of unionism that was even more dismissive of workplace concerns than the business union model it claimed to replace.

Likewise, the worker-center model does not focus on building organization on the shop floor. Workers' centers often focus on legal remedies such as fighting unpaid wages. Relying on publicity strikes, these workers' centers attempt to pass protective labor legislation such as $15-an-hour minimum wage or improving laws against wage theft. Unlike traditional unionism, workers' centers are not based in particular worksites; nor do they seek to organize particular shops. Now, my point isn't to knock this work, but these forms of activism are not unionism.

We have previously discussed how class struggle unionists favor shop floor struggle and organization. But even traditional business unionism, however bureaucratic, favored a shop union structure. Most unions have shop stewards, negotiate over workplace issues, and have a structure that at some level allows for input of workers. Unionism should flow upward from the shop floor. Traditional union theory holds that workers should elect their own leaders, formulate their bargaining demands, and pick their strike issues. The reason is because the workers alone know what matters to themselves. It also means that workers should decide for themselves who should go on strike.

We routinely hear calls for strikes of entire industries by foundation-funded nonprofits that do not represent more than a handful of workers in an industry. Traditional unionism had elaborate procedures for calling strikes and boycotts, including votes of the workers involved as well as authorization from other parts of the labor movement who would be bound to support the actions. While this can be dismissed as bureaucracy, and if often became that, the purpose was to ensure the workers losing pay or risking their jobs on a solidarity strike got a say in their livelihoods and futures. Yet labor liberal foundations think nothing of putting out a call to shut down Uber nationwide or for all fast-food workers in a city to strike with no vote of the actual people who will be losing paychecks.

Class Stand

Class struggle unionists are outsiders who view government institutions as lined up against us. In contrast, labor liberals are the ultimate insiders—operators in the left edges of the Democratic Party. None of their tactics challenge the capitalist system, and in fact, most push us farther into the system's embrace. Class struggle unionists view the system as rigged, whereas labor liberals believe they are smart enough to play around the edges.

Central to the labor liberal project is building left-liberal influence in the political arena. In part, this can be hard to see since they have co-opted strike action. Take Fight for $15, for example. They use strikes as publicity demonstrations to get media coverage to help influence public opinion in order to pass legislation. In this scheme, workers are essentially props in support of a legislative agenda. Now, while the results may be laudable, it is more like the work of politicians or progressive organizers than trade unionists. They appropriate the language and tactics of the labor movement, without the labor movement's core worker involvement, worker control, and workplace focus. Doing so muddies the water and does not help push forward class struggle unionism.

Whereas class struggle unionists view the government as an instrument of class rule, labor liberals view the government as a protector. So they propose reform of labor law such as card check for union elections, mandatory arbitration of first contracts, and strengthening the role of the National Labor Relations Board. As discussed in the previous chapter, a hallmark of class struggle unionism is a distrust of the government, which is seen as the protector of the system of private ownership of the means of production, and controlled by corporate interests.

Recently, labor liberal commentators, often centered in elite law schools, have advocated an elaborate scheme of government-regulated industry bargaining. Often combined with mandatory arbitration, it would have the government play a large role in labor relations. But this emphasis on the government as protector is at odds with class struggle unionism's belief that government structurally favors our opponents.

Law professor Matthew Dimick argues that the labor movement should focus on expanding freedoms rather than, as the labor liberals suggest, rights that would be vindicated by some government agency or court. Dimick notes because courts can pick and choose the limits of acceptable activity, "rights are used to curtail workers' concerted activity."[15] But Dimick observes that a strong, class-conscious labor movement is built on worker self-activity: "Strikes and other concerted activities are not merely means by which workers achieve gains in the workplace. Rather, they are moments in the process by which workers constitute themselves as a class—building solidarity, raising class consciousness, creating their own norms and institutions, and discovering their own forms of class power."[16]

Labor liberalism promotes a brand of unionism heavily dependent on the government and courts to protect labor rights. But if you live by the sword, you die by the sword.

But on a deeper level, we need to discuss what kind of labor movement, and society, we are trying to build. As Dimick says,

In the end, the judgment of a good labor law should not be whether it serves the immediate interests of particular workers or even groups of workers. The question, instead, should be what kinds of labor law will permit the working class to forge itself into the most cohesive, inclusive, and self-conscious class for itself, capable of independent and autonomous action. Only a fight for labor freedoms can obtain that goal.[17]

Building a strong militant workers' movement requires breaking with labor liberalism.

Despite its overall weaknesses, one of the strong points and indeed much of the attraction of labor liberalism is its rejection of narrowness. Since business unionists seek only to represent a limited set of workers and often tie their fate to particular employers, they can fall into a narrow unionism that says screw the rest of the working class. Labor liberalism, to its credit, rejects that approach. But it often does so more from the perspective of middle-class social movements than from a unionism rooted in the workers' movement.

The next chapter will discuss how class struggle unionism is a better perspective for those who want a broad, inclusive labor movement. Class struggle unionists ground the push for a broad labor movement in the struggle against the billionaire class. That way, we have a militant, antisexist, antiracist labor movement that believes in fighting on the shop floor, union democracy, and sharp class struggle.

Chapter 4

Class Struggle Unionists Fight for the Entire Working Class

Some workers are in professional occupations, such as nurses and journalists, while others may be factory workers or waitresses. Some workers live in the United States, while others live in countries such as India or Tanzania. But despite the differences they share the common experience of having to work for others, who keep the products of their labor, to survive. For that reason, class struggle unionists have long fought against racism and sexism in the labor movement and society at large, rejected the pro-corporate foreign policy of the US government, and fought for class-wide policies and politics.

A defining feature of business unionism is a narrow focus on the interests of a group of workers in a plant or craft. This leads to a conservative form of unionism that tries to get limited gains for a handful of workers while ignoring the rest of the working class. This plays into the hand of the billionaires who rely on keeping workers divided to maintain their system of exploitation.

Class struggle unionists, in contrast, believe in something bigger, and frankly more inspiring. Seeing labor's struggle as part of a broader working-class conflict, they link labor struggles with other fights. They fight for the unemployed, for single-payer health care, and for issues benefiting the entire working class. But it also means that class struggle unionists fight against attempts to divide the working class, such as racism, sexism, and anti-immigrant policies.

Antiracism

The fight against racism is central to class struggle unionism in the United States. The United States was founded on slavery and maintained by white supremacy for hundreds of years. We cannot have class struggle unionism that does not put antiracist struggle at its core. Racism pervades all aspects of the labor market in the US. White workers make 30 percent more than Black and Latino workers. For Black women, the situation is even worse, with over 20 percent of Black women living in poverty.[1] Racism pervades our workplaces, from hiring patterns to job classifications and to who gets singled out for discipline. This difference in employment leads to fundamentally different work experiences.

Wealth is also racially based in this country, where the "median Black family, with just over $3,500, owns just 2 percent of the wealth of the nearly $147,000 the median White family owns."[2] Black home ownership is 44 percent compared to 73.7 percent for whites.[3]

The history of the labor movement on issues of race is horrible. The American Federation of Labor allowed international unions to exclude Black workers, the union label was born out of racism against Asian workers, and well into the 1960s and beyond, many AFL and CIO unions operated under racist policies. As one scholar who has studied the role of race and labor concluded, "While the differences of skill, ethnicity, and gender have proved surmountable, the project of working-class organization has repeatedly foundered on the shoals of racism."[4]

The labor movement did not shed discriminatory practices easily. It took a combination of outside pressure in the form of civil rights legislation combined with a generation of civil rights struggles within the unions. In her book *Black Freedom Fighters in Steel*, labor studies professor Ruth Needleman recounts how decades of Black steelworker activists fought to gain access to better jobs in steel plants.

Well into the 1980s and beyond, unions of firefighters, building trades, and others supported hiring and promotion practices that continued gender and racial discrimination. Even today the far right of the labor movement includes police unions and the border guards who still use unionism as a shield for white supremacy. In recent years with the rise of the Black Lives Matter movement against police brutality, many have criticized the role of police unions in the labor movement. Studies have shown that police unions are a key opponent of structural changes to reduce police brutality. The business unions, including the AFL-CIO, have mouthed support for Black Lives Matter but refused to take on police unions.

For these reasons, it is inconceivable to speak of class struggle unionism without antiracism at its core. We cannot build a strong labor movement by dodging questions of discrimination.

Class Struggle Unionism Puts
Fighting Racism at the Forefront

Decades before the labor movement was forced kicking and screaming to desegregate in the 1960s, class struggle unionists were pushing for a union movement that welcomed all workers. The AFL in the early 1900s was organized around craft union lines that excluded the vast majority of industrial workers, including immigrants who were concentrated in the developing mass-production industries. Many unions, such as the International Association of Machinists, refused to allow Black workers to join. And where African American workers did join unions, they were confined to the worst, lower-paying jobs.

In the early 1900s, the Industrial Workers of the World developed in large part due to the racist and exclusionary practices of the American Federation of Labor. The IWW opened its doors to all workers and offered a different path for the labor movement on race. The IWW even attempted to establish interracial unionism in the Deep South, while at the time the AFL unions were mired in white supremacy. In Philadelphia in the early 1920s, the IWW established an interracial local that for over a decade was able to maintain control of the Philadelphia docks on a class struggle union basis.

Antiracism and representing the entire working class was a hallmark of class struggle unions. The left-led unions with strong influence from the Communist Party from the 1930s through the 1950s stood out for their strong antiracist practice. Robin Kelley's now classic *Hammer and Hoe* tells the history of the Communist Party in Alabama during the 1930s, where, fighting incredible repression, these activists sought to organize southern African American tenant workers.[5] As discussed later in this chapter, their antiracism allowed them to build a powerful labor movement in the Deep South.

This commitment to interracial unity helps explain the CIO's ability to organize industries such as meatpacking and auto. Rejecting segregation, the activists adopted a form of interracial unionism that did not paper over race issues. The meatpackers had long kept out unionization by dividing the groups by race. This racial division of the workforce not only harmed generations of Black workers, but it also undermined the struggle for unionism. During the packinghouse strikes of the early 1900s, employers consciously sought to pit Black workers and white workers against each other. They provided white workers with access to higher-paying jobs and better communities in order to divide the workers.[6]

But in the 1930s, the Communist Party helped organize meatpacking by taking on race issues directly. "First, in the mid-1930s, a core alliance of union militants took shape. The nucleus was comprised of three major groups: Communists who were relatively new to the industry, skilled veterans of earlier organizing campaigns, and black activists who had been in the plants since the late 1910s and early 1920s."[7]

After their successful organizing, the unions continued to make antiracism central to their unionism. During World War II, "they used their newly acquired power to attack remaining manifestations of in-plant discrimination such as hiring bars, restrictions on promotion, and the existence of lily-white departments."[8] With a strong base in the workplace, the union was able to expand into a community force on race issues.

The Communist Party labor activists won the confidence of Black activists in meatpacking due in large part to the party's strong record fighting the Jim Crow terror in the South. During the 1930s, the party prioritized the struggle against racism, working to fight issues such as the white-supremist terrorism used to prop up the system of racial exploitation in the South. At the core of white-supremacist terror were both judicial violence and extrajudicial violence in the form of lynching.

The Communist Party picked up defense of the Scottsboro Boys, nine young Black men who were framed and sentenced to death for allegedly raping two white women in March 1931. The case garnered international attention due to the work of party members. As Robin Kelley explains in *Hammer and Hoe*, Communist organizers "transformed a local—and, I might add, common—injustice into an international cause célèbre by building a mass movement to free the Scottsboro Nine. . . . They formed Scottsboro defense committees all over the country, whose members flooded the Alabama governor's office with telegrams, letters, and postcards demanding freedom for the Scottsboro Boys."[9]

The work included creating massive rallies in US cities and support groups in Europe, and it "reversed the poles of criminalization, turning young black men—and young working-class white women—into victims and the state into the criminal."[10]

This work in the community tied into multiracial organizing in the Deep South, including incredible work of organizing Black sharecroppers and later steelworkers in Birmingham. Unlike the AFL's policy of capitulating to southern racism, class struggle unionists understood that building multiracial working-class solidarity meant directly confronting white supremacy.

This strong antiracist unionism helped propel forward a generation of African American union leaders through their work in class struggle unions. Leaders such as Ferdinand Smith of the National Maritime Union played a major role in the burgeoning civil rights movement, bringing Black working-class voices to a movement long dominated by Black professionals. The key point here is antiracism was not an afterthought or slogan but central to the class struggle unions' identities.

One of the strengths of the class struggle antiracism of the Communist Party in the 1930s was they saw class and race as the key forces capable of changing society. In previous chapters we discussed how class oppression is only one of the types of oppression in society, and that others include race, gender, and immigrant status. But race and gender cut across class lines, meaning one can be a small-business owner and be discriminated against in access to credit because you are Black or female.

The working class is where race, gender, and class intersect in society. Given the racial stratification of the class, this is specifically true of the lower-paid sections of the working class. This leads to a couple of distinct tasks: within the labor movement the task is pushing to make antidiscrimination a priority, and within other social movements fighting racism and sexism, the task is pushing for working-class issues to be addressed.

An excellent and more recent example of this is the incredible organizing done by Black Workers for Justice in North Carolina. Formed in 1982 out of a struggle against discrimination in hiring at Kmart stores, BWFJ organized Black workers in the workplace and fought discrimination in the community. The BWFJ mission statement articulates their role:

> BWFJ believes that African American workers need self organization to help empower ourselves at the workplace, in communities and throughout the whole of US society to organize, educate, mobilize and struggle for power, justice, self-determination and human rights for African Americans, other oppressed nationalities, women and all working class people whether employed or unemployed, union workers or unorganized. We work to build the strength and leadership of Black workers in the Black Freedom and labor movements.[11]

This provides for a powerful alliance rooted in the working class.

Class Struggle Unionism
Fights Gender Discrimination

One of the other great divides within the working class and society is discrimination based on gender. A class struggle unionism that seeks to represent all members of the working class must fight oppression based on gender. Discrimination based on gender impacts working-class women in numerous ways. A discriminatory labor market pays women less than men and undervalues unpaid work by women.

In the first chapter we discussed how the billionaire class views workers as just another input into the production process. To them, workers are not human beings but rather materials to be used in production. And like every input into the production process, they try to drive the cost of workers down so they can make more and more money.

One way of doing that is by shifting the burden of childbearing and child-rearing onto women in the form of unpaid work. Rather than the reproduction of a labor supply being the job of society as a whole, it gets shifted from the billionaire class to the working class, predominantly upon women.

Now, it may seem strange to talk about human beings as an input into production. But we have to remember, the billionaires do not care about workers as people but only for the labor the working class supplies. Thus they attack social programs, oppose pre-school programs, and seek to privatize education and turn it into a profit-making area. They are against family welfare programs and programs like Social Security that take care of workers after the capitalists have used up their bodies through a lifetime of toil.

As a direct result of sexism and the devaluation of their work, women make only 82 percent of what men make.[12] Like race, the labor market remains segregated by gender with male occupations consistently paying more. Thus jobs like construction pay far more than child care and health care. Gender oppression interacts with race oppression, with Black females making only sixty-one cents on the dollar compared to males.[13]

This difference can be attributed to a number of factors including discrimination in the value of work and women being forced to work part-time or absent from the workplace due to child-rearing responsibilities. Part of a class struggle approach must be directly dealing with these inequities.

For class struggle unionists this means that we need to prioritize the fight for programs that shift the burden off of women, such as paid family leave, continuous medical benefits, and social programs to support children and families. But it also means opposing the division of labor in society as a whole by standing against sexism. Merely focusing on narrow bargaining demands does not work if the society as a whole remains unequal.

Class Struggle Unionism Is True Social Unionism

Many progressive unionists identify as social unionists or social justice unionists. Social unionists argue unions should work with community groups and embrace broad social demands. This is an incredible draw, especially given the narrowness of much of the existing labor movement. Social unionism has pushed the labor movement to take better positions on immigration, to confront issues of racism, and to form alliances with other social groups. For public employees, social unionism leads to a form of unionism that emphasizes ties to the community. All of that is good stuff, as far as it goes.

Social unionism first gained popularity in the United States in the mid-1990s based off the experience of unionists who built a powerful labor movement in countries such as Brazil, South Africa, and the Philippines. These struggles were characterized by a high level of workplace militancy and an approach that emphasized fighting for the whole working class. In the framework of this book, that perspective would fit squarely into the class struggle outlook.

However, US social unionism deviates significantly from its roots in militant third world unionism. Within the broad tent of social unionism are staff-driven projects that form alliances with nonprofits and foundation-funded workers' centers that look to the

Democratic Party. But the term *social unionism* is also used to describe efforts with widely varying approaches, encompassing solid class struggle unions such as the Chicago Teachers Union. As labor scholar Kim Scipes has noted, "This creates the basis for a great deal of confusion among labor theorists and writers, as well as unionists: people coming from different perspectives can use the exact same term to describe completely different things—and without even knowing it."[14]

Some commentators have attempted to distinguish between true social unionism and top-down social unionism, promoting terms such as *corporate social unionism* or *social unionism from above*.[15] The problem is it's hard to see any of those distinctions gaining traction. For these reasons, we should reject the term *social unionism* to describe our framework.

The problem with the term *social unionism* is not what it includes—we should all agree that a broad class-based approach is good—but what it fails to include. As a framework it misses sharp class-on-class struggle, connection to the workplace, union reform, and the like. Yet those are hallmarks of most of the actual activists who employ the framework, such as teachers in cities such as Los Angeles, Chicago, and elsewhere.

Class struggle unionism is a better term to describe this work as it has all of the strengths of social unionism and none of the baggage. Class struggle unionism captures all the positive elements of the social unionist approach but adds in a member-driven uncompromising unionism. Another way to think about this is all class struggle unionists are social unionists but not all social unionists are class struggle unionists.

Class Struggle Internationalism

Capitalism is a global system reaching into every corner of the globe, transforming economies and subordinating entire nations to the needs of capital. At the top of the heap is a handful of billionaires. According to the relief agency Oxfam, a mere twenty-six people own more wealth than half the world's population. Yet, almost three and a half billion people are living on less than $5.50 per day.[16]

Just as capital spreads across the planet, so does the global working class. Economist and labor educator Michael Yates estimates that there are 3.5 billion members of the global workforce with several more billions either vulnerably employed or unemployed.[17] Many work for the same multinational corporations and perform similar functions, and as we discussed previously, all have to sell their labor to survive.

This system of global capitalism is an integrated system of global production. General Motors operates plants in thirty-five countries, with 173,000 workers worldwide. A given car may have components from multiple countries. Global corporations view workers as commodities, which means that they are undifferentiated inputs into the production process. Obviously, the billionaire class does not care what country they come from, except the cheaper they can buy the labor the better.

For unionists this means a couple of things. First, true internationalism means forging worldwide alliances. The labor movement needs to adopt the same international perspective that our enemies hold. We have more in common with workers in other countries than with the owners of industry. Capitalism knows no boundaries and neither should we. Class struggle unionists are true internationalists.

For US unionists, this gives us multiple tasks. In order to maintain our standards, we must forge ties directly with other global workers to effectively combat capital. After decades of experience it is clear that true global labor solidarity will not come through business unionism. The official channels of international business unionism are ineffective and bureaucratic.

But it also means confronting the foreign-policy establishment, something that the labor establishment is not good at. In the international arena, just like at home, the foreign policy of the US is largely dictated by corporate interests. Major international institutions such as the World Bank and the International Monetary Fund use financial power to dictate policy in poor countries. When necessary, US military power is used to back up corporate interests.

US corporations are able to exploit cheap labor around the world by supporting authoritarian antilabor regimes. For unionists in the United States, especially in industries that compete internationally, this provides a downward drag on wages. The lack of labor rights directly affects our bargaining standards. This means we must oppose US foreign involvement and military intervention, which serves corporate interests.

Class struggle takes different forms in different places. Because their repressive governments brutally repress labor rights and multinational corporations exploit the resources of their countries, unionists often cannot rely on mere union activity because their US-backed governments kill unionists and help corporations plunder the resources of their countries.

Sometimes entire countries rebel against the power of international corporations. But countries that do this come under incredible pressure. In one example out of many, for generations workers and peasants in Central America suffered under oppression from US-backed dictatorships. These dictatorships brutally repressed workers who tried to form unions or push for any democratic reforms. When workers and their allies in countries such as Nicaragua or El Salvador rose up against the US-backed regime, they faced economic sanctions, military intervention, and interference by the US Central Intelligence Agency.

When these countries rebel, the US media, the government, and the war establishment join in to attack them. For those who have gone through strikes, you will know what it feels like to have the establishment join up to attack you. The establishment's attack on a rebelling country, however, is exponentially fiercer than its attack on strikers, because it is not just one union taking on one employer but a country taking on the system of global capitalism.

Business unionism has a horrible record on international affairs. For decades, from the red purges of the 1950s into the 1990s, the AFL-CIO operated on an extreme anticommunist agenda that favored US government and corporate interests over workers. Kim Scipes has written extensively about the collaboration of the AFL-CIO with the US Central Intelligence Agency in suppressing labor rights around the world, concluding:

> One, the U.S. Government has seen Labor's foreign policy program as an important tool to keep workers around the world generally immobilized, a key project in trying to maintain stability within countries of the U.S. Empire. And two, the foreign policy leaders of the AFL-CIO recognize their importance to maintaining the U.S. Empire, both acquiescing in the foreign policy program's use and, whenever possible, actively participating in the process of maintaining the U.S. Empire.[18]

As Scipes notes, the AFL-CIO leadership to this day has not come clean about its role in undermining labor rights around the world.

During the 1980s, the United States government waged a war against left-wing governments in Central America. While the AFL-CIO supported the US government, many class struggle unionists in the 1980s bucked official AFL-CIO policy to back the rebels and oppose US intervention in El Salvador and Nicaragua.

When John Sweeney and the New Voice leadership took over the AFL-CIO in the mid-1990s, they changed the name of the AFL-CIO's government-funded organizations to the Solidarity Center. But while they changed the name and some of the worst practices, the funding by the US government continued. Today, the Solidarity Center gets 90 percent of its funding from the US government. One of the unanswered questions is how can the US government, including the anti-union Trump administration, be funding pro-worker operations?

US corporations have shown no regard for American workers, by shifting jobs overseas, supporting union-busting regimes, engaging in wars to support corporate America, and more. But in international affairs, corporations and the government demand absolute loyalty from business unions. And they typically get it. For this reason, one of the dividing lines within the labor movement has been international affairs.

When class struggle unionists have stood for internationalism, they have faced heavy reprisal. During World War I, even though by many accounts the IWW tried to keep its nose down and focus on economic demands, they were ruthlessly repressed. Socialist Party leader and unionist Eugene Debs spent years in jail, running for president from his jail cell and getting nearly a million votes. As Debs declared, "Let me emphasize the fact—and it cannot be repeated too often—that the working class who fight all the battles, the working class who make the supreme sacrifices, the working class who freely shed their blood and furnish the corpses, have never yet had a voice in either declaring war or making peace. It is the ruling class that invariably does both. They alone declare war and they alone make peace."[19]

During and after World War II, questions of foreign policy were used to destroy the influence of class struggle leadership. The Trotskyist leadership of the Minneapolis Teamsters local was put on trial for sedition during the war. In the 1950s, the Cold War between the United States and the Soviet Union was used to attack class struggle unionism.

In recent decades, class struggle–oriented unionists have attempted to revive the tradition of working-class internationalism. The United Electrical Workers union developed a decades-long relationship with the Frente Auténtico del Trabajo in Mexico, an independent class struggle–oriented union.[20] The effort included rank-and-file exchanges and joint work opposing destructive trade agreements such as NAFTA. The UE also has a strong record of opposing US wars abroad.

Previously we discussed how class struggle unionism comes into conflict with business unionism. Because class struggle unionism disrupts and rejects the policy of accommodation with capital that business unionists prize, they come into conflict. Likewise with foreign policy, because business unionism lines up with international corporations against the workers of the world, class struggle unionists who support true internationalism have come under fire by the labor establishment. Independent politics, which we will discuss next, is another flash point.

The Struggle for Immigrant Rights

The domination and disruption of economies by US corporations displaces millions of workers in poor countries in Latin America, Africa, and Asia. As their economies are reshaped to serve the needs of foreign corporations rather than domestic needs, millions of workers are displaced. On top of that add US-backed wars, and millions of workers want to move to have a better life.

The billionaires claim they are for free trade, and they secure the free movement of goods and capital around the world through trade deals such as the North American Free Trade Agreement and the Trans-Pacific Partnership. But these are one-sided deals that allow capital to roam the world searching for the cheapest labor while confining workers to single countries.

Class struggle unionists see all workers as part of a global working class standing up to multinational corporations and a global billionaire class. The flip side of the internationalism discussed above is supporting the struggle of immigrant workers in the United States. Fighting against anti-immigrant bias is part of class struggle unionism.

As with issues of race in general, the record of business unionists on immigration has been horrible for most of labor history. In the early 1900s, the American Federation of Labor used racist language to trash foreign-born workers. A major reason class struggle unionists formed the Industrial Workers of the World is because the AFL refused to organize the largely immigrant emerging mass-production industries. Rather than being a symbol of solidarity, the union's label was born in California in the 1880s as a racist, anti-Chinese-worker organizing tool. Well into the 1980s, the AFL-CIO took anti-immigrant positions on national legislation.

One of the ways the rich maintain power is by dividing the working class, and one of the easiest groups to target is immigrant workers. On the one hand, corporations love having a sizable pool of workers with few labor rights whom they can intensely exploit. But when these workers demand rights, employers use the threat of deportation to attempt to stop organizing.

Preceding the rise of Donald Trump was a right-wing movement attacking immigrants in Arizona and other border states. When Trump was running for office in 2016, building the border wall and attacking immigrants was a key part of his message. But it soon merged into a general support of white supremacy, which is a main feature of the anti-immigrant movement.

Immigrant workers are a key part of the labor movement. Many immigrant workers come from countries such as El Salvador where there are strong traditions of class struggle unionism. Indeed many of the bright spots of the labor movement in recent decades have been centered in immigrant communities. Although many outside the labor movement routinely call for general strikes, the one group capable of actually involving thousands or even millions of workers in general strikes has been immigrant workers.

Immigrant workers are concentrated in many strategic industries. Many industries such as non-union residential construction and meatpacking have seen a massive switch to immigrant labor. This is not a result of immigrant workers taking jobs but rather a result of the busting of unions and the transformation of these jobs into low-wage, high-risk occupations.

For all these reasons, the fight for immigrant rights must be a key component of class struggle unionism.

Class Struggle Politics

In many countries around the world, labor movements have formal or informal ties with political parties that explicitly challenge the system of wage exploitation. Some of these parties are labor parties that support nationalization of certain industries, and others are socialist parties that seek to establish a system free from private ownership of income-producing means of production. Regardless, these parties uphold the idea that a workers' movement needs a political movement that is free from the influence of the billionaire class and is solely dedicated to defending the interests of the working class.

In the United States we do not have such a party, setting aside the minor parties that garner few votes—we have the Democratic Party. The Democratic Party is not a labor party or a socialist party, and it does not challenge the system of exploitation discussed in this book. The party receives significant funding from the owners of industry. Not surprisingly, the policy orientation of the party reflects this elite influence.

Class struggle unionists believe that the labor movement needs class struggle politics, which is completely free from the influence of the employing class. Some advocate that we need our own labor party, while others support the Bernie Sanders / Alexandria Ocasio-Cortez wing of the Democratic Party. But many others believe we should not focus on politics at all but build a powerful labor movement at the point of production. Regardless, class struggle unionists understand that to build a powerful labor movement we must break free from the stranglehold that the Democratic Party has over the labor movement.

Prior to the 1930s, labor learned from bitter experience that the government is not a neutral force. Samuel Gompers, the conservative head of the AFL, understood better than many of today's progressive unionists the problems that workers had trying to get justice in the current system. Gompers noted,

> The mass of the workers are convinced that laws necessary for their protection against the most grievous wrongs cannot be passed except after long and exhausting struggles; that such beneficent measures as become laws are largely nullified by the unwarranted decisions of the courts; that the laws which stand upon the statute books are not equally enforced; and the whole machinery of government has frequently been placed at the disposal of the employer for the oppression of the workers.[21]

What Gompers was referring to was the long history of labor unions struggling for years to pass labor legislation only to see the legislation undercut by pro-corporate judges.

Recognizing this, a section of class struggle unionists rejected the idea of unions getting ensnared in politics of the labor or socialist stripe. Many conservative AFL unions under Gompers's leadership subscribed to a philosophy of volunteerism, which meant they tried to keep the government out of labor relations. But even among class struggle unionists, the issue was divisive. This issue dominated the conventions of the IWW in the early 1910s, where the majority of activists argued for a syndicalist view that prioritized workers' strike activity, up to and including a general strike. A minority within the organization saw socialist political action as key.

With the great labor upsurge of the 1930s, a section of corporate America saw the importance of a softer approach to the labor movement. With four hundred thousand workers engaged in sit-down strikes in 1937 alone, a policy based only on brute force was not working. With the passage of the National Labor Relations Act, a system of government tolerance of unions came into being.

In the 1930s, a subset of Congress of Industrial Organization leaders began to favor incorporation into the liberal state. Foremost among them was Sidney Hillman, the social-democratic leader of the Amalgamated Clothing Workers of America. Hillman favored strong ties with the Roosevelt administration, in contrast to CIO and United Mine Workers leader John Lewis, who favored political independence.

Coming out of the 1940s, the labor movement tied its fate to the Democratic Party. Labor officials became major players at national Democratic Party conventions and dutifully urged their members to vote for party candidates. Rather than rely on the self-sufficiency of the 1930s militancy, labor officials came to see the Democrats as protectors. During this period, liberal theorists talked of a tripart pluralist scheme of governance where technocratic government officials, labor, and management ruled the economy.

The problem with this view is it failed to take into account the underlying structure of the economy. As Frances Fox Piven and Richard Cloward noted in their classic study, *Poor People's Movements*, in our society the real source of power is hidden: "Power is rooted in the control of coercive force and in control of the means of production. However, in capitalist societies this reality is not legitimated by rendering the powerful divine, but by obscuring their existence [through] electoral-representative institutions [that] proclaim the franchise, not force and wealth, as the basis for the accumulation and use of power."[22]

To translate into lay terms: in the billionaire economy we get to elect our rulers.

. Many critics of the labor movement's alliance with the Democratic Party point to the lack of results. Because the Democratic Party receives significant funding from corporate America, most politicians tend to not step on the toes of the funders. Now, if you see the working class and the employer class locked in battle, this presents obvious problems.   •

This elite influence and funding of the Democrats not surprisingly pays dividends for the billionaire class. Despite the fact that polls repeatedly show the American people want real health-care reform, fair trade policies, and climate protections, the national Democrats are known for half measures. Allying with Democrats often means the labor movement comes down on the side of the billionaires rather than the working class.

Indeed some of the biggest attacks on the labor movement in recent decades have come from conservative Democrats. Bill Clinton pushed through the North American Free Trade Agreement, which decimated manufacturing unions and is estimated to be responsible for a net loss of seven hundred thousand manufacturing jobs in the United States and constituted a downward drag on the remaining firms.[23] Jimmy Carter pushed through deregulation of trucking and airlines, leading to devastating hits to the unions in those sectors. The billionaire movement that seeks to privatize public education invests heavily in Democratic politicians. Too close of an identification with the Democratic Party disarms labor unions in fighting these attacks.

In terms of enacting labor's priority of labor law reform, the Democratic Party has a horrible record. During the last fifty years we have seen four Democratic presidents: Carter, Clinton, Obama, and Biden. In the Carter administration, narrow legislation to address construction worker compensation concerns went nowhere, as did a broader labor law reform bill in 1978 with little support from Carter. Between NAFTA, cutting government jobs, and the failure of striker replacement legislation, the Clinton administration was a disaster for labor. According to one analysis, "The Clinton administration is usually viewed as being even worse for labor than the Carter administration—the miserable end product of a long decline in the quality of the labor/Democrat relationship."[24]

But locked into a two-party system, the business unionists believe they have nowhere to go. As bad as the Democrats are, the Republicans are seemingly worse. But unwilling to employ the militancy necessary to build independent union power, business unionists are left with little choice but to rely on Democrats. In 2016, the labor movement spent an estimated $167 million on the elections along with an incredible amount of time and effort of staff and members.[25] Despite this incredible outlay of cash, labor was outspent by just five billionaires: Tom Steyer, Sheldon Adelson, Donald Sussman, Fred Eychaner, and Dustin Moskovitz.

The labor liberals, for all their fiery talk, are little better, and probably worse in terms of lack of independence from the Democrats. Despite their fake one-day publicity strikes and press events, their core orientation is pressuring progressive Democrats to enact protective social legislation. Even more than the business unionists, they need the Democratic politicians who are core to their strategy.

Now, one could argue that putting millions of dollars and countless volunteer hours into a party that constantly betrays labor's interests is a waste, and one could argue that if that were it, while bad, labor could deal with it—after all, we waste money on all kinds of things. But that's not it; the close reliance on the Democratic Party allows the ideas of the billionaire class into the labor movement. Rather than the class struggle ideas discussed in chapter 2, the alliance with the Democratic Party encourages moderation, support of US corporate foreign policy, and cooperation with and a reliance upon the very government that is set up to protect the billionaire class. It is a conservatizing force and offers an alternative to labor militancy. This is far worse than a mere wasting of resources on elections, as it sets a wrong direction for labor.

In chapter 5 we will discuss the need to develop a labor movement capable of violating labor law. But despite all evidence to the contrary, the leadership of unions still holds out hope that someday they can elect Democrats and reform labor law. Even though this will never happen, it is a way of avoiding labor's crises. This applies to both business unionists who look for labor law reform and perhaps even more so to the labor liberals who dream of government-mandated sectoral bargaining or legislated minimum wages.

Even worse, this alliance with the Democrats is used as a kind of outlet valve. When sharp struggle flares up, the business unionists are frequently caught off guard and are not in control. Typically, they try to divert struggles back into the safe haven of electoral politics.

This was certainly the case with the Wisconsin uprising when week after week thousands of Wisconsinites showed up at the state capitol. The uprising against Republican governor Scott Walker's law gutting public employee bargaining in the state drew hundreds of thousands of rank-and-file union members to surround the state capitol for weeks, while thousands occupied the capitol rotunda. It was one of the more inspirational union events of the past decade. Union leaders were caught off guard, but as the struggle subsided they pushed members to simply focus on recalling Walker and electing Democrats rather than expanding the struggle. Likewise in the wake of the red state teacher revolts, the national unions attempted to get striking teachers to put their effort into electing Democrats.

Chapter 5

Class Struggle Tactics

A strong labor movement requires tactics capable of winning strikes, securing gains for workers, and bringing management to their knees. In the absence of winning tactics, we can talk tough and go for a strident social unionism, but we'll be forced to make the same compromises as the business unionists.

The starting point of a discussion of tactics is recognizing how grim the situation is for unions today. The labor movement represents only six out of a hundred workers in the private sector, and there are no signs that will change anytime soon. Entire industries—once union strongholds such as trucking—are largely non-union. There is no realistic prospect of reorganizing these industries.

Although in recent years we have seen an increase in strike levels, they are mainly concentrated in the public sector and low by historical standards. While it is a welcome development it does not, as some commentators suggest, signal a revival of the labor movement.

In 2018, driven mainly by teachers' strikes, the total number of striking workers in major strikes—which is defined as strikes over one thousand workers—was the highest since 1986. In 2019, strikes by autoworkers at GM helped drive another high level of strike activity compared to recent decades. But the vast majority of strikers in these years were public employees.[1] While public-sector strikes are very important, they don't face permanent replacement of striking workers and have the advantage of being able to pressure public officials who have a level of accountability that private corporations lack in the United States.

Comparing these numbers to historical averages, it is clear we have a long way to go in reviving the strike. In the 1980s, an average of eighty-six major disputes of over one thousand striking workers took place per year. And these numbers were down from the hundreds of major strikes per year in the 1950s and 1960s, representing tens of millions of lost workdays. In 1986, there were eleven million lost workdays. In 2019, there were a little over three million lost workdays.

The reason for the decline is simple. As I along with many other authors and law professors have discussed elsewhere, labor law is completely geared toward employers. Employers are allowed to legally permanently replace striking workers, workplace-based solidarity is largely outlawed, and employers can easily get injunctions against mass picketing. As much as organizers hate to hear it, we simply cannot win within the framework of existing labor law.

We have four decades of trying to revive the labor movement within the bounds of existing labor law. It is not working. There is no point in mincing words. We need to focus attention on building a wing of the workers' movement capable of violating labor law. Truly reviving the strike in the private sector will require radical action of a type not seen in the labor movement for decades, involving a wholesale repudiation of existing labor law, a rejection of employer property rights, and a commitment to organize the key sectors of the economy through militant tactics.

No one says this will be easy. Last century, it took advocates over forty years to move the labor movement to industrial unionism. From Eugene Debs's efforts to build an industrial railroad union in the 1890s to the formation of the IWW in the early 1900s to the many countless battles at AFL conventions, the effort for industrial unionism was a long-term effort. We need a left wing of the labor movement that has a similar long-term view.

Some folks may say this is pie in the sky. But the real illusion is that we can win within a system set up for our unions to fail. We have one hundred years of history to show that working people make substantial gains only when they struggle to break free of imposed legal limitations. There is zero chance that we can revive unionism within existing labor law, and the prospect for meaningful labor law reform is equally dim.

So in this chapter we are going to flip labor theory on its head. For decades, we have been trying to fit our labor strategy within a fundamentally unjust labor law. Here, we will determine which tactics can win strikes and then discuss how to force the system to live with our successful labor tactics.

How to Win Strikes

We know all we need to know about winning strikes. It's really not that complicated and has been spelled out in detail in classical union theory, which I explain in detail in *Reviving the Strike*. Simply put, a successful strike must impede the profit-making ability of the employer by preventing either the production or distribution of products and services. And in certain industries, unions must be able to counteract employer measures such as plant relocations or closures.

Successful strikes begin by understanding that production and distribution processes are divided into three parts:

1. Any enterprise requires inputs into the production process such as buildings, capital to operate, and raw materials.

2. All enterprises require a process where human labor provides services or produces goods. This is where value is added.

3. All enterprises require delivery or distribution of their services or products.

An effective strike impacts one or more of these categories, thus preventing the employer from making a profit. It's really that simple.

Additionally, labor strategy must include tactics of solidarity capable of producing industry-wide agreements, preventing the employer from closing down the plant or shifting production to a non-union area, and preventing the undercutting of union wages by non-union competitors. As discussed previously, in an era of international commerce such a strategy must be internationalist in nature. These considerations have all been spelled out in detail in classical union theory and were once considered commonplace among both labor activists and theorists.

It is important to note that the strike strategies for public and private sector are fundamentally different. I have discussed this issue in detail in my book *Strike Back*, but public employee strikes are fundamentally political. The points above primarily relate to private-sector strikes, which must stop production or otherwise economically impact an employer.

1. Stopping the Input of Goods or Services

In order to run the enterprise, the employer needs various inputs into the production process. This could be raw materials, human labor, plants and facilities, or capital to purchase all of the above. If the right combination of these inputs is cut off, the enterprise cannot function, the employer cannot make a profit, and the strike can be won.

Now, depending on the input, there are a limited number of ways to prevent the employer from obtaining the necessary materials or input:

- Mass picketing to physically block supplies from going into a plant—for example, blocking railroad tracks to stop a shipment of coal into a plant
- Getting truck drivers to honor picket lines, not in the limited way of today, but by completely stopping the delivery of goods
- Striking or blockading related businesses that supply the employer
- Cutting off capital to operate, which would require using secondary strikes or boycotts to go after banks and other funders

The point here is to cut off the lifeblood of the business.

2. Stopping the Work Process

This category of tactics involves preventing production. In the old days, one could simply withdraw skilled labor or could convince replacement workers not to scab. But for the most part, preventing labor required blocking scabs from entering the workplace or, alternatively, occupying it.

Alternatively, workers could strike on the job or conduct quickie strikes in which they did not cede control of the workplace. The goal of these tactics is to stop the employer from operating the workplace. The key tactics involve a degree of coercion to prevent nonunion or disloyal union workers from scabbing on the strike.

3. Preventing the Distribution of Goods and Services

The third category involves a set of traditional union tactics centered around stopping the sale or distribution of goods or services. Again, there are a limited number of tactics. A general consumer boycott could try to stop the sale of the struck goods, although these are very difficult to sustain. Much stronger are secondary strikes and boycotts in which the targets are merchants who sell, transport, or distribute the struck goods. The basic concept is if an employer produces goods or services but cannot sell, deliver, or perform them, then all is for naught.

The Power of Solidarity

The final piece of the puzzle is solidarity—labor's greatest strength. Historically, labor was able to standardize wages across employees and industries by utilizing tactics of workplace-based solidarity, including secondary strikes, industry-wide strikes, and in exceedingly rare instances localized general strikes. Beyond requiring powerful strikes, unionists understood that to provide stable collective bargaining it is necessary to standardize wages across entire industries. This helped deal with problems of runaway shops, the rise of nonunion competitors, and a variety of ills.

This is an abbreviated discussion of strike tactics. For a more detailed discussion of tactics, please see *Reviving the Strike*. And for public-sector strikes, including extensive discussion on confronting labor law, please see my book *Strike Back*.

Reestablishing Militancy

Now, observers will notice that all of the most effective tactics mentioned above have been outlawed by what I refer to as the system of labor control. This is a set of laws and court rulings that outlaw traditionally successful trade union tactics.

- Stopping inputs into the plant interferes with property rights of employers, may run afoul of secondary boycott provisions, and will provoke NLRB intervention.
- Stopping scabs from entering plants violates both judicial injunctions and state laws on trespassing.
- Most effective solidarity tactics have been outlawed by the Taft-Hartley Act.

Simply put, in one fashion or another every vehicle for successful unionism has been effectively shut off. We also know that labor law is not going to be amended to allow these tactics, and even if it were, the courts would undermine the legislation.

So all of this means that our key task is to develop a labor movement based on militancy and violating labor law. Establishing militancy will require a complete break with our existing union practices, conflict with institutions and officials who do not want to fight, and a completely different worldview. Reestablishing militancy requires a number of steps that will be discussed in more detail below:

- Developing a theory of labor rights that justifies militancy
- Creating new forms of worker organization
- Orienting toward the rank and file
- Establishing concrete intermediate steps to build a militant labor movement

We have decades of weakness—law-abiding, rule-following, unimaginative, losing unionism—such that we can't even see what winning looks like. In an era of weakness and decline, folks tend to think small and look for strategies that can make a little progress. But often that is exactly the wrong thing. Breaking free requires thinking big.

So far in this chapter we've mainly discussed what we are up against: a system of labor laws put in place to thwart successful unionism and a legal system ready to bankrupt unions that step outside the box. Our task then is to figure out how to break free.

For far too long we have tried to be the left edge of the possible instead of expanding the range. But when folks do break beyond current limitations, such as the Occupy movement or the red state teacher revolt, that is when great things happen. It's time to set our sights higher. We need to ask ourselves some questions: What would a labor movement capable of violating judicial injunctions look like? What would it take to organize entire industries? What sort of resources and support would we need? What sort of ideas would labor activists need to hold? What would be the incremental steps to get us there? Once we answer these questions, we can begin to construct the type of labor movement we need. What we will likely find is that this will not be business unionism or labor liberalism but rather class struggle unionism.

Combatting repression begins, first and foremost, with the battle of ideas. To defeat employers, we need to get their ideas out of our heads. To reestablish militancy, we need an entirely different approach to labor organizing, to our theory of labor rights, and to our conceptions of unionism. In other words, it requires a complete break from the framework established by liberal labor law and with labor liberalism.

Underlying the system of labor control is a set of relations that privilege private property rights over human need. Political scientist Alex Gourevitch has written at length about how the ideas underlying successful unionism come into conflict with the existing order.

> American labor law does not just place enormous and unfair constraints on the exercise of labor rights because of Supreme Court

mischief, employer assaults on the Wagner Act, or historic distortions of the Constitution. Those constraints also reflect some basic truths about liberal morality and the nature of power in a capitalist society. Liberal societies do not permit private actors to interfere with others' exercise of their basic civil and economic liberties. In a capitalist society, those basic liberties necessarily include freedom of contract, private property, and managerial authority.[2]

Effective unionism strikes at the core values of capitalist society. Whereas the predominant set of ideas in society are based on individual profit, unionism is based on the collective good. That's why these class struggle ideas are so important on a very practical level.

It would be a mistake to underestimate what we are up against. Once we move past symbolic civil disobedience and move into labor militancy, we rapidly come into sharp conflict with the existing order in a number of ways:

- By blockading or taking over workplaces, we are directly challenging the property rights of employers.

- By disobeying injunctions, we are defying the judiciary and setting our movement up as a parallel force in society.

- By blocking scabs from entering workplaces, or defending ourselves against police attacks, we are engaged in actions that will be deemed violent.

- By interjecting ourselves into the employment relationship, we are directly challenging the process of capital accumulation.

- By rooting our struggle in a fight for control of the workplace, we struggle against exploitation at its source and challenge the basic structure of employment.

- By utilizing industry-wide or general strikes, we engage in overt class-wide struggle that breaks free of the notion we live in a classless society.

All of these actions are deeply destabilizing to the system. Corporations and the government will attempt to either crush or co-opt such actions. Combating those employer strategies requires the class struggle ideas discussed in previous chapters.

Take mass picketing, which was indispensable in reviving the modern labor movement. Legal scholar Ahmed White notes that

> mass picketing is, by the lights of liberalism, an insufferable mode of labor protest. For it is at once highly effective in arming workers to challenge the interests of capitalists, and also steeped in threatening visions of unmediated class conflict and worker solidarity and charged with the prospect of violence. For these reasons, the tactic has never been much defended by liberal jurists, academics, or other commentators. As the history of its treatment at the hands of courts, legislators, police, and commentators of all kinds makes clear, mass picketing is, in a word, anathema to a liberal system of labor law and policy.[3]

To be clear, these tactics would be opposed by Democratic and Republican judges and politicians alike.

As Alex Gourevitch points out, these effective strike tactics are considered coercive under liberal thought:

> What this means is that the majority of workers, who are relatively easy to replace, often have to use some coercive tactics if they want to go on strike with some reasonable chance of success. These tactics either prevent managers from hiring replacements, prevent replacements from taking struck jobs, or otherwise prevent work from getting done. The classic coercive tactics are sitdowns and mass pickets.[4]

This sets up an irreconcilable conflict between liberal labor theory and militancy. After all, what gives us the right to coerce others?

This is exactly why we need a class struggle ideology. In the preceding chapters we discussed the elements of class struggle unionism, including the need to

- reject the billionaires' control of the economy,
- promote intense class-on-class struggle,
- develop grassroots unionism rooted in the workplace,
- challenge the entire capitalist system, and
- establish a class-wide form of unionism.

Together this set of ideas forms the basis for countering the power of liberal ideas and reestablishing militancy. Breaking free from the system of labor control requires class struggle ideas. Perhaps the most important idea is solidarity, which is why escalating and broadening disputes is essential.

It is important to note that these ideas differ from the prevailing labor thought of recent years, which mainly center on unions taking progressive positions on political questions. In order to have class struggle tactics our labor thought needs to become a lot more radical.

Injunctions and State Power

Historically, when labor has responded with militancy, we have had to confront repression from the government, condemnation from the corporate press, and the biased "black robed" defenders of capital—judges. From the jailing of socialist union leader Eugene Debs for his role in the Pullman strike to the 1914 Ludlow massacre to mowing down strikers and their families in the 1937 Little Steel strike, the rich have been ruthless in protecting their untold wealth. So any strategy based on militancy must deal with the issue of state and employer repression.

Ahmed White has studied employers' use of violence in great detail in labor history, including a book about the Little Steel strike called *The Last Great Strike: Little Steel, the CIO, and the Struggle for Labor Rights in New Deal America*. One of the relatively rare defeats for labor in the 1930s was the campaign of the Steel Workers Organizing Committee to organize a group of companies called Little Steel. The giant US Steel had reached an agreement to recognize the union after seeing the sit-down strikes in auto. But Little Steel, which included Republic Steel, Inland Steel, and Youngstown Sheet and Tube Company, held out against unionization. The group was anything but little and vehemently anti-union.

Like other scholars, White notes that questions of violence and coercion are central to any strike.

The essential purposes of picketing—especially the mass picketing—were to coerce scabs from entering the mills, draw out those who remained inside and ultimately prevent the company from running the plants. . . . For their part, the companies were quite willing to use force to push through the picket lines, intimidate picketers, and provoke them and thus undermine the legitimacy of the cause while paving the way for legal intervention.[5]

The essential problem unions face is that in order to win a strike, the union must be able to forcibly stop scabs. But when they do, employers paint the actions as violent and use force themselves or get the government to intervene.

Like many of the strikes of the 1930s, the Little Steel strikes started off with mass picketing at plants in the South Side of Chicago and Youngstown, Ohio. Thousands of picketers surrounded plants, prepared to starve the employers out. The employers, however, were prepared to go into battle. The congressional La Follette Committee investigated in the wake of the strike and "determined that during the strike, the Little Steel companies in Ohio and Michigan were backed by 3,600 armed men (not counting the National Guard), of which nearly 2,000 were under their direct control."[6]

During a peaceful demonstration that would come to be known as the Memorial Day Massacre, Chicago police fired on the crowd, killing ten and injuring many others. Unlike many of the other battles of the 1930s that were under the leadership of class struggle unionists, the top-down Steelworker leadership failed to escalate the dispute. With the government intervening to break the picket lines, the strike was eventually lost.

Contained within this battle are the essential points of union activity. To win the strike, the union could not simply picket; they needed to stop production, which meant using some level of force to block scabs or supplies from entering the plant. Yet when they did exercise those tactics, they were branded as violent and the government came in to break the strike.

In the Little Steel strike, in contrast to the other strikes of the period, the conservative top-down leadership of the Steelworkers

International folded in the face of the injunctions, rather than fight their way through the dispute. Business unionists, when confronted with this dilemma, typically choose to back down and forgo the use of picket line militancy. While this prevents state repression, the strike is then lost.

This happened during the Little Steel strike, but it also happened in the great strikes of the 1980s where workers employed militancy, such as at Hormel, Pittston Coal, Phelps Dodge, and others. In all these strikes, grassroots workers tried to stop production or expand the strikes. And in all situations, they were shut down by conservative national union leaders. It's not that often workers do not instinctively know how to win; the problem is that winning tactics quickly get shut down.

The strategy employed by the Little Steel companies was called the Mohawk Valley Formula, named after a plan popularized by James H. Rand of the Remington Rand corporation. According to White,

> Rand's formula consisted of no fewer than nine steps, all oriented to employing threatening armed forces, spies and provocateurs, company-sponsored back-to-work movements, and staged reopenings to terrorize and demoralize strikers, provoke them to violence, and discredit them; then using the specter of violence and pretense of a 'state of emergency' to mobilize opposition to the strike on the part of local police and the courts.[7]

This Mohawk Valley Formula includes a couple of key elements. The first is a highly ideological propaganda element geared up to paint the union as violent outside agitators and demoralize the strikers. The second is to legitimize the use of force against strikes in order to restore "law and order."

This seems to put unions in a no-win situation. If we do nothing, the employer will win the strike because production will continue. If we engage in militancy, the employer will get an injunction and stop the strike. Unions must reject this false choice and change the story line.

Employers today have things a lot simpler. During the 1930s, they needed to set the unions up before they could get the state to intervene. Eighty years of union weakness have atrophied our movement and emboldened employers and judges. Now all an employer needs to do is go to court with a video or two of rowdy picket lines and get an injunction limiting picketing to one or two members per gate. Our ability to resist injunctions then depends on how we respond. If we comply with the injunctions we will likely lose the dispute. To dispute the injunctions we need a class struggle ideology that will justify disobedience, but we also need a set of practical tools to confront the injunctions.

Confronting Injunctions

Today perhaps the central question for the labor movement is how to deal with injunctions against effective union activity. Unions face crippling legal damages for violating injunctions. Employers can sue unions for damages under section 301 of the Labor Management Reporting and Disclosure Act (LMRDA). Unions can be fined for violating judicial injunctions and be subject to the RICO racketeering statute or other suits. These fines can pose an existential threat to unions.

We have plenty of examples in recent years of injunctions:

- In 2015, Walmart received sweeping injunctions in multiple states, forbidding flash mobs on stores that were tame by historical standards, even though the protests only briefly interrupted shopping.[8]
- In 1999, the pilots' union at American Airlines was fined $45 million for an alleged sick-out.[9]
- In 2019, American Airlines received an injunction forbidding mechanics from refusing to pick up completely voluntary overtime.[10]
- In 2019, a $93.6 million judgment was levied against the International Longshore and Warehouse Union for engaging in a slowdown against an operator in Portland.[11]

- In 1994, United Mine Workers of America was fined $64 million for the 1989 Pittston strike, although this was reversed by the US Supreme Court on procedural grounds.[12]

All of these injunctions are backed up with the threat of fines that could cripple the unions.

The very threat of these injunctions is effective at curtailing militancy. Many international unions hold assets numbering in the tens or hundreds of millions. These unions represent hundreds of thousands of members in various industries and would put that money at risk by violating injunctions. Moreover, full-time union officials depend on the union for continued employment. Whether they admit it or not, there are very real pressures on union staff and officials to not face crippling fines.

As British labor scholars Ralph Darlington and Martin Upchurch have noted, the concern among union staff about injunctions is just bread-and-butter unionism:

Rank-and-file workers are obliged to sell their labour power to an employer, and their immediate material interest is bound up with ensuring they get the maximum possible return for that sale. By contrast, while union officials also depend on a money wage, this is something that is gained from a *union*, not from an employer. The official's very existence is indissolubly connected with the existence of the unions.[13]

So if the union goes out of business, the union officials would no longer be employed. That is a powerful incentive to dampen militancy.

Darlington and Upchurch, in their analysis of the striking experience in Great Britain, determined that "employment laws in Britain have struck at the official's Achilles heel, with the fear that unlawful strike action by their members might lead to court injunctions, damages of tens of millions of pounds and the sequestration of union funds resulting in their repeatedly calling off threatened action."[14] Given the hesitancy of US unions to engage in militancy, it is clear the same process is working here.

We know from several decades of experience that the existing labor unions will be unwilling to confront injunctions. As British labor scholar Richard Hyman remarked, "Those in official positions in unions possess a direct responsibility for their organization's security and survival, a role encouraging a cautious approach to policy. In particular this is likely to induce resistance to objectives or forms of actions which unduly antagonise employers or the state and thus risk violent confrontation."[15]

It does not matter how militant the union leaders are or how reform-minded. Few are going to put their unions at risk.

It is important to note this is not simply a case of self-serving bureaucrats. Preserving assets and existing bargaining relationships is a legitimate concern of any union leader. Putting the entire union at risk is not something done lightly. In addition, without a movement or philosophy validating such an approach, it is a lot to expect from union leaders. So any class struggle unionism strategy will need to deal with this issue.

For established unions, the question of militancy is fundamentally a question of protection of union assets. The problem of having large treasuries is not a new one for the labor movement. One way unionists have dealt with this is to simply not have assets. In his book *Radical Unionism*, Ralph Darlington notes, speaking of the 1920s, that "syndicalists everywhere refused to build up large strike funds or to provide unemployment, sickness and death benefits for members and their families . . . to avoid amassing of a large treasury in the hands of a centralised union bureaucracy that might develop its own interests remote from the members and attempt to oppose strikes."[16]

For existing international unions that is not an option, but start-up unions without assets would not be similarly vulnerable.

In *Reviving the Strike* I discuss a 2004 proposal by the American Federation of Teachers to organize new industries based on a strategy of militancy and creating new independent organizations. It is time to have a renewed discussion about that proposal.

Similarly, organizing in new areas such as high tech, insurance and banking, public and private sector employers in the South and West, manufacturing transplants, etc., may require creating new unions from scratch and even adopting unconventional tactics unencumbered by the restraints of current labor law. Existing unions have much to risk and lose through the purposeful violation of Taft-Hartley (secondary boycotts and shutdowns, sit-down strikes, etc.); organizing committees of start-up unions with no accumulated treasuries or bricks and mortar might enjoy greater strategic and tactical flexibility and would have substantially less to lose through the smart and strategic use of unconventional approaches where appropriate. The AFL-CIO could explore the legal and financial avenues for building institutional firewalls for donor unions (or for the AFL-CIO as a donor organization) that would be responsible for providing money, logistical assistance, long-term loaned staff and other help without the expectation of an organizational quid pro quo.[17]

Now, one may ask why the labor movement did not act on the AFT proposal. For one, most unions are content to merely survive. They go from one contract to the next, with little interest in grand plans.

But we also have an entire nonprofit industry of groups organizing employers outside of the formal union structure. There has been the whole Fight for $15 effort to organize fast-food workers and an effort to organize Walmart workers by OUR Walmart. But many groups lack independent funding and don't operate on a class struggle union basis. In order to actually organize entire industries, any such independent organizations would need to be free of all outside interference and provided the funding and latitude to wage sharp class-on-class struggle. It would require a completely different ideology, function, funding, and structure than the existing alternative organizations.

Conducting these types of militant actions would require breaking with the dominant liberal ideology. This is something that few in the labor movement are willing to do, and it is why in my book *Reviving the Strike* I note that conservative labor leaders of generations ago were more oppositional to the system than today's labor left.

The Importance of Escalation

But even if we do have independent organizations, or militant unions, willing to confront injunctions, the question becomes, how we can possibly do that without confronting employer repression to win strikes? Employers can count on the police, the courts, the corporate media, politicians, and even the National Guard if need be. Beyond that, they have an entire system in place that paints them as the law-abiding ones by virtue of their ownership of the means of production.

The key lessons we learn from both victories and defeats in labor history is the importance of escalating disputes by bringing in more and more workers. One of the great victories of the 1930s was the Flint sit-down strike, where autoworkers took over the plants at General Motors to win unionization. After the company obtained an injunction against the strike, instead of backing down, autoworkers took over Chevrolet plant number 4.

Likewise, during the longshore workers' strike of 1934, escalation at a key point in the struggle helped win union contracts for thousands of West Coast longshore workers. When San Francisco police fired on pickets on July 5, killing three strikers and supporters, many unions would have backed off. Instead, led by class struggle militants close to the Communist Party, the union leadership opted for escalation. Rather than backing down to the repression, thousands of strikers marched in a funeral procession. Local unions passed resolutions in favor of a general strike, and 150,000 workers struck. The strike concluded shortly after that.

In the game of poker there's a phrase "raise or fold." More often than not, raising to put pressure on your opponent typically is the correct play, as opposed to passively calling. As the saying goes, poker rewards aggression. Passively calling is rarely the correct strategy, and in that case, one might as well consider folding and choosing another battle. The same holds true with bargaining and strikes.

When we compare successful strikes throughout history versus failed strikes, often it will boil down to a key moment: did the union try to tone things down by getting sucked into government mediation efforts, or did they fight through the difficulties? Certainly in the key battles of the 1980s, most unions backed down rather than expanding the strike.

The more workers involved in the dispute the more costs to our enemies for responding with repression. We know this from the red state teacher revolts of 2018. Teachers in states such as West Virginia, Oklahoma, and Arizona went out on illegal statewide strikes. Yet because they struck statewide, they did not face legal repercussions or discipline. The sheer size of the conflict provided striking teachers protection.

During the 2018 West Virginia teachers' strike, an old mineworker gave the teacher activists a good piece of advice: "Go all in or nothing." The advice proved sound—if teachers had struck in only one district, they likely would have been fired. But by all going all in together it was impossible to replace them all, plus it magnified their political impact.

This experience is consistent with the lessons of the public employee upsurge of the 1960s. Strikes were illegal in every jurisdiction in the United States until the late 1960s, yet public employees engaged in one of the biggest waves of civil disobedience to win their unions. Millions of teachers, sanitation workers, and others successfully violated labor law to win strikes during this period.

In my book *Strike Back*, I detail the incredible lessons of this period. To summarize a few,

- Public employees believed in their right to strike.
- Public employees had broad public support.
- Workers engaged in militant action and escalation if necessary.
- Workers discovered there was no such thing as an illegal strike, just an unsuccessful one.

From the 1960s' public employee rebellion we learn that even though employers have guns, power, and the law on their side, policy makers typically hesitated to use repression because of worries it would end up drawing sympathy for the workers and make the dispute harder to settle.

Chapter 6

Class Struggle Organizing, Rank-and-File Unionism, and the Militant Minority

Over the last decade we have seen important battles between labor and the billionaire class with a return of strike activity, particularly among teachers. The mass social movements of Black Lives Matter, the electoral manifestation in the Democratic Socialists of America, and the popularity of socialist ideas show the possibility of struggle. With the development of a new stage of militancy, increased contradictions in society leading to openness to left and socialist ideas, we have the chance to build a new and fundamentally different labor movement.

Doing so will require uniting folks around a class struggle union approach. Believing in class struggle unionism is not enough. Unless we develop a trend within the labor movement that embraces these ideas, they will remain just that—good ideas. This raises a whole set of questions: Should we work in conservative business unions or establish new forms of organization? What is the role of middle-class socialists in the labor movement? Should folks take jobs on staff or rank and file? How should union militants relate to the union bureaucracy? Should the focus be on fighting the boss or reforming the union? How should we relate to progressive union officials?

These questions cannot be answered piecemeal but are best approached in what can be called a class struggle organizing approach. There are three major components to a class struggle organizing approach:

- A program to put the labor movement on a class struggle basis
- A method of transforming the labor movement
- A set of organizational techniques to accomplish the above

All of this adds up to a very different mode of labor organizing from what we practiced for the last few decades. It puts class struggle ideas in command, relies on inspiration rather than technique, and seeks conflict rather than creating organization.

In each of the previous chapters we contrasted a class struggle union approach from the labor liberal approach. Likewise, in this chapter on organizational questions we find a distinct historical class struggle approach to transforming the labor movement.

Putting the Labor Movement on a Class Struggle Basis

The core of a class struggle approach is to build a labor movement based on class struggle principles. Labor activists Bill Fletcher and Fernando Gapasin put this in blunt terms in their 2009 book *Solidarity Divided*: "We are not interested in perpetuating illusions: the reality is that, absent an alternative, transformative trade unionism, the United States will see no labor renewal. Rebuilding the AFL-CIO, or even creating a new federation, will have been an exercise in futility unless we get to the roots of the problems facing organized labor."[1]

The authors argue that to revive trade unionism we need a more comprehensive critique of unionism. Yet in the absence of a class struggle framework, for the last decade activists have focused on pieces of a correct strategy: new methods of organizing, union democracy, socialist electoral politics, and the like. Even my previous books focused on reviving the strike and militancy with less focus on the comprehensive viewpoint necessary to accomplish that. We need the whole package: an explicit analysis of the billionaire class, a class-wide approach, class struggle ideology, and class struggle tactics. But we also need a plan and program to build a labor movement on those ideas.

Today, many have simply given up on the labor leadership. Rather than demanding bold plans to organize industries, labor activists set up workers' centers, organize small shops, or believe they can organize workers through sheer willpower. It is a strategy that says we can do it ourselves. But it places no demands on national leaders of unions. Unlike generations past, we do not propose militancy, an end to class collaborationism, or the use of the institutional power of the labor movement to take on capital.

The problem with the small-ball approach is it lets the labor bureaucracy off the hook. It makes the crisis of labor one of organizing techniques rather than a failure of a workers' movement capable of waging class struggle, leaving tens of millions of workers out of the picture. This is the equivalent of promoting personal financial self-help as the response to the austerity economy. In contrast, previous generations of class struggle unionists demanded a labor movement capable of confronting capital on a grand scale. We need to think about what it would take to either transform the existing labor movement or build a new one, or both.

Previous generations of class struggle militants took a dim view of the existing labor movement. The IWW called the AFL the "American Separation of Labor," referring to its narrow, exclusive craft organization, and called bureaucrats "labor fakers." Similarly in the 1920s, William Z. Foster railed against the labor corruption, labor capitalism, and narrowness of the AFL.

Likewise left unionists of the 1970s saw themselves as organizing the rank and file against the union bureaucracy. Characteristic of the time, in his popular book *False Promises*, Stanley Aronowitz pointed the finger at union bureaucrats.[2] Targeted in this critique were both the openly corrupt officials but also more common and damaging phenomena such as lazy overpaid business agents, staff who had contempt for line workers, and a class collaborationist approach to dealing with management. Labor officials were viewed as a key impediment to union reform.

While the 1970s labor activists prioritized reforming unions and building rank-and-file struggle independent of and in opposition to the labor bureaucrats, in recent years we find less emphasis on taking on the labor bureaucracy. With union density at 6 percent in the private sector, we don't have a powerful labor leadership to critique. But even more, the politics of labor liberalism allow for progressive views without requiring a challenge to the labor leadership.

Historically, class struggle militants had a vision to transform the entire labor movement based on the application of class struggle ideas. In the words of Micah Uetricht and Barry Eidlin, their "ideological vision informed their unionism, making it militant, dynamic, and powerful."[3] There was a core connection between their views of the economic system and their concrete program to change the labor movement.

Looking at historical examples can make things clear. In the 1920s, the labor movement was in desperate shape. Although production was shifting away from craft to industrial manufacturing, the AFL stubbornly stuck to their old ways and refused to organize on an industrial basis. Rather than fight, AFL officials fell for labor-management cooperation schemes, set up labor banks and other businesses, and engaged in much corruption.

William Z. Foster, the leader of the 1919 steel strike and a labor leader in the Communist Party, headed up the Trade Union Educational League, which had an ambitious program to put the labor movement on a class struggle basis. The policy statement of the group stated, "The Trade Union Educational League proposes to develop unions from their present antiquated and stagnant conditions into modern, powerful labor organizations, capable of waging successful war against capital."[4]

The plan to move the labor movement forward was central to TUEL's strategy. Specifically, they proposed the rejection of class collaborationism and adoption of class struggle, industrial unionization, organization of the unorganized, the shop delegate system, and creating a labor party.[5]

TUEL activists in each industry then developed plans specific to their industries. So in the rail industry, concentrations of TUEL members supported amalgamation of the rail unions and opposed the Railway Labor Act. In other industries they put forward specific agendas based on industrial unionism and sharp class-on-class struggle.

In the auto industry, TUEL began publishing shop newsletters written in a rank-and-file manner and agitating for class struggle tactics. "In the 1920s and 1930s Communists in auto were the main voices on behalf of industrial unionism and class struggle,"[6] according to historian Roger Keeran, who studied the incredible influence of the Communist Party in auto in the 1930s. Keeran noted the Communist Party had tireless organizers and disciplined groupings. But he also zeroed in on the importance of their programmatic ideas.

> Communist influence also stemmed from the correspondence of their ideas to the aspirations of auto workers and to the requirements of unionization. The ideas of industrial unionism, unity of all auto workers, aggressive strike action, and rank and file control provided a far more realistic blueprint for unionization than the AFL's craft unionism, avoidance of strikes, reliance on government mediation, and control from the top down.[7]

They combined class struggle ideas with an overall plan to move labor forward.

Similarly, Farrell Dobbs, the Trotskyist organizer of the 1934 Minneapolis truckers' strike, explains the steps in putting the Minneapolis Teamsters local on a class struggle basis:

> First they had to battle their way into Local 574, which had jurisdiction over the coal yards in which they were employed. Steps could then be taken to convert the union into an instrument capable of serving the workers' needs. Policies based on revolutionary class consciousness could be introduced. Rank-and-file militancy could be channeled into a showdown fight with the

trucking employers. Conservative union officials who failed to meet the test of battle would begin to lose influence over the membership.[8]

Dobbs shows that the politics of class struggle unionism were systematically employed to go into battle with employers and in the process transformed the union. This systematic plan led to the success of the truckers' strike, but it also moved on to transform the Minneapolis Central Labor Council and contribute to organizing trucking in the Midwest.

During the decades leading up to the 1930s, groups such as the IWW, the Western Federation of Miners, and others pushed a program of labor militancy, industrial unionism, racial unity, and strike action as the way forward for labor. Although they were great organizers, activists, and strike leaders, they also put forward a vision of how to take on capital on a grand scale.

This element is missing from much of today's labor commentary. Unlike class struggle unionists of decades past, progressive unionists today place few demands upon national unions. In the absence of a realistic plan to move labor forward based on a class struggle approach, we are left with ineffective solutions.

- We can elect more militant leaders but can supply no guidance for how they will behave differently once in power.
- We can build alternative unions or organizations, but without tactics capable of taking on capital they end up being marginal to class struggle or foundation-funded nonprofits.
- We can move from fad to fad such as alternative unions or bargaining for the common good, but we will not have challenged the fundamental shortcomings of modern unionism.
- We can perfect organizing techniques, but without a class struggle policy we are left with simply being better organizers or more committed activists.

Overall, much of today's labor commentary on union revival sees the problem as organizing techniques or organizational form rather than a fundamentally different approach to class struggle. This is killing the labor movement.

In the 1970s and 1980s, most left-wing groups put forward concrete plans to fight back against the burgeoning anti-union offensive. A vibrant left wing offered an alternative way forward for the labor movement based on class struggle principles. Labor activists aggressively pushed an anti-concessions line, opposed the "Team Concept" model of labor relations and other labor-management cooperation schemes being forced upon autoworkers, fought US military intervention against left-wing governments, and supported reform movements within the unions. Their approach was oppositional in character and explicitly based on left-wing class struggle politics.

Over time, however, many of these activists put their politics in their pockets, abandoning class struggle unionism in favor of labor liberalism and accommodation with the bureaucracy. There were likely a number of reasons for this. By the early 1980s, most Marxist groups had imploded, and many adherents had abandoned class struggle theory. Many of the ex-leftists approached the labor movement on a very practical basis, leaving theory to the law professors and labor liberal staff. On the one hand, this was good because they rejected the sectarian excesses of the 1970s. However, many essentially abandoned class struggle unionism, which is the only hope for the working class.

In part, this can be attributed to the relative weakness of the anticapitalist left during this period. With the waning of the great social movements of the 1960s and the rise of neoliberal ideas, left-wing and socialist ideas were marginalized within society as a whole, including other social movements. It is not surprising that the labor-movement left mirrored the weakness of the left overall.

In addition, the labor movement in the 1980s was fiercely anticommunist. Left-wing or class struggle politics were ruthlessly suppressed. Class struggle unionists were red-baited and had little opportunity to express explicitly socialist politics. So, many learned to keep their politics to themselves and adopt frameworks that fit better within the existing context. But with the increasing popularity of antiestablishment and socialist ideas today, now is the time to challenge neoliberal ideas in our movement.

For decades we have allowed the liberal law professors and the labor education crowd to dominate the discussion of labor strategy. With the increasing receptivity for socialist ideas among younger folks and labor activists, we have new opportunities for discussion of class struggle ideas. It's time for class struggle unionists to take the lead.

The starting point is to realize what we are up against. Labor activists by definition are optimists—how else do you motivate people? The problem is, without a realistic estimate of the conditions we face, it is hard to develop a sufficiently radical response. But revolutionary optimism alone is not enough. Missing are the systematic and withering critiques made by previous generations of labor leftists.

The minimum necessary elements of a class struggle program today must include a plan to organize the key sectors of the economy, establish international solidarity, and revive militant labor tactics capable of bringing capital to its knees. Such a strategy must include both demands on unions and workers' centers and independent class struggle initiatives. Of course, having the perfect ten-point program is not enough, so it requires concrete organizing, struggles within unions, and strike activity.

Class Struggle Organizing and the Militant Minority

Folks who believe in class struggle unionism are few in number compared to the entire labor movement. We must be able to expand our reach within a union, a city, and the labor movement as a whole. One can have great ideas, but without a way of putting them into action, they are just ideas.

The militant minority, which developed as a way of dealing with the weak and ineffective AFL craft unions last century, is seen by many in today's labor movement as key to labor's revival. Micah Uetricht and Barry Eidlin, in a comprehensive review of militant union strategy, determine that "this group was key not only in leading upsurges but in consolidating their gains. Today's labor movement largely lacks this militant minority. We argue that rebuilding it is central to labor revival."[9] In a similar vein, Charlie Post notes that "without a layer of workers with a vision and strategy for how to organize, fight, and win, labor officials have been free to pursue their near-suicidal approach."[10]

As a method of organizing, the concept of the militant minority is pretty simple. Organizers and activists know that normally there is a core of people who most want change in a workplace and a community. A good organizer pulls those folks together and engages the enemy, whether it be the boss or slumlord, and in doing so systematically pulls more and more people into the struggle.

Now, to be clear, the key point to the militant minority strategy, as discussed above, is putting the labor movement on a class struggle basis. It is not just an organizing technique. It is fundamentally an oppositional strategy geared toward transforming the labor movement.

The militant minority strategy, originally developed by French syndicalists as a way of transforming their conservative unions, was imported to the United States by William Z. Foster. Foster, who later joined the Communist Party, became convinced that a key weakness of the American labor movement was the policy of creating pure or left trade unions isolated from the main labor federation, the American Federation of Labor. Foster, after joining the Communist Party in the early 1920s, helped establish the Trade Union Educational League as a vehicle to put the US movement on a class struggle basis.

Labor historian Philip Foner details the steps TUEL laid out: "The first drive was to take place for the purpose of establishing local educational groups of militants in every trade and in all important cities and towns. Once established, these local groups would, in addition to their other activities, perform the vital work of carrying out the efforts to organize the militant in the respective industries."[11]

Following that, TUEL activists would organize in an industry such as rail and work for amalgamation.

TUEL suffered from too close an identification with the Communist Party and was ruthlessly suppressed by AFL bureaucrats. Nonetheless, this relatively small group was able to engage in significant struggle during a period where confusion and retreat prevailed. In the 1930s, with the working class on the move, the strategy proved very effective.

The Industrial Workers of the World had a completely different view of working with the AFL, which we will discuss below. Yet the IWW shared a larger viewpoint of a militant labor movement based on an explicit class struggle approach.

The left groups in the 1970s drew inspiration from the militant minority strategy and established caucuses that emphasized pushing struggles on shop floor issues or contract negotiations. One of the groups, the Revolutionary Union (RU)

> directed members to get jobs in factories (or hospitals, post offices and other nonindustrial settings with large numbers of workers). In a dozen or so cities RU cadre launched local anti-imperialist newspapers aimed at workers—*The Milwaukee Worker*, *The People's voice in Detroit*, etc.—and usually was able to establish small "intermediate workers organizations" around these publications.[12]

Drawing together groups of workers at the grassroots, developing a program through communications, and fighting on issues are key to the militant minority.

In discussing the militant minority, William Z. Foster made clear that he saw this group as not just organizers but class fighters. According to Foster,

> The fate of all labor organization in every country depends primarily upon the activities of a minute minority of clear-sighted, enthusiastic militants scattered throughout the great organized masses of sluggish workers. These live spirits are the natural head of the working class, the driving force of the labor movement. They are the only ones who really understand what the labor struggle means and who have practical plans for its prosecution.

Touched by the divine fire of proletarian revolt, they are the ones who furnish inspiration and guidance to the groping masses. They do the bulk of the thinking, working and fighting of the labor struggle. They run the dangers of death and the capitalist jails. Not only are they the burden bearers of the labor movement, but also its brains and heart and soul.[13]

To unpack it, Foster focuses on the militants who are the inspiration and who understand the plan to fight the bosses. They are the heart and soul of the struggle, willing to risk jail. They are the class fighters.

Those who have been involved in struggles know what I mean. Through the process of fighting, new leaders step forward. During strikes, the strike committees are often composed of new folks who then form the militant minority. Some people talk about the militant minority as if it preexists in the workplace. But it is something that is built through struggle.

Now to a certain extent, there are some workers who are more militant by experience, learning, or happenstance. But as Rick Fantasia points out in *Cultures of Solidarity*, solidarity is created in a process.[14] In fact, who constitutes the militant minority may very well depend on what the issue or struggle is. For groups who put issues of gender or racial oppression at the core of workplace struggle, the militant minority may look different than a standard union-reform effort. In general, the militant minority is the section of a workplace, a union, or the broader labor movement who want to fight. This conception of organizing is quite different from popular versions today.

Labor Liberal Organizing

Today's labor activists spend a lot of time and energy on how to organize workers. At the center of organizing are techniques employed by skilled organizers, with much emphasis placed on techniques and skills such as mapping the workplace and structure tests in which the workers are judged as to whether the organizers believe they are ready to strike. Under this framework, middle-class activists are tasked with organizing the whole working class. Although folks may disagree on how to do this work, the underlying framework is rarely questioned.

Now, organizing skills matter, but left-wing trade unionism is not fundamentally about skills; it's about putting trade unionism on a class struggle basis. We have entire industries unorganized, we don't have enough resources, there are labor laws that prevent successful union strategies, and there is almost zero push for the militancy required. Better organizing techniques cannot resolve any of this. Not to be too harsh on today's labor activists, but perhaps less organizing would be required if we actually had strategies that made sense to workers.

Previous generations of militants played more of an ideological role within the workplace and the union. It's not that they were not organizers, but they saw their role as taking on management and union bureaucrats unwilling to fight the bosses. For me, this has been less a point of skilled organizing than taking a hard line with management and pushing within unions to fight. The role of class struggle unionists is to help bring the working class into battle—to promote class struggle.

But labor liberals see themselves as the indispensable workplace organizers. Knowledge of course is power, and when you are the ones who know how to organize, you have the power. Above all, labor liberals are the experts. They are masters of the organizing campaigns and of systems of rating workers for union support during the organizing campaigns. Many leftists concentrate within organizing departments of unions (and research, education, and political affairs). They devise elaborate public relations strategies with their communication expertise at the center of them, rather than building actual class power in the workplace.

Class struggle unionists, in contrast, set up a different practical and ideological pole within a workplace or local union. Whereas labor liberals see themselves as the organizers, class struggle unionists see themselves more as fish in the ocean. Class struggle unionists seek to integrate with the working class and help spur action. Class struggle unionists are agitators, oppositionists, and strategists. As William Z. Foster notes of the militant minority, it is "'the little leaven that leaveneth the whole lump.'"[15] For those who don't bake bread, including myself, that means the ingredient that helps activate the others. The labor liberals, in contrast, view themselves as the chefs.

Class struggle unionists believe in the capacity of workers to organize themselves. Think of the great upsurges of recent years: the Wisconsin uprising, the red state teacher revolt, the Occupy movement. Folks are actually quite creative about organizing themselves if given the space. Class struggle unionists seek to create that space for workers, while labor liberals seek to fill it.

Key Questions for Class Struggle Unionists

Class struggle unionists do not agree on all questions. We disagree on how much to focus on reforming existing unions versus creating new ones, how much effort to put into electing new leaders, the role of electoral politics, and a wide variety of questions big and small.

Advocates of the class struggle union approach come out of different political tendencies. No one has all the answers, and it is important that folks keep an open mind. One of the mistakes that left-wing labor activists made in the 1970s was thinking they knew all the answers, engaging in sectarian behavior, and refusing to work with other groups. In reality, this was a form of elitist intellectualism imported into the labor movement that set our movement back greatly.

One of the concerns in writing a book about class struggle unionism is the far, far left wing (we call them ultraleftists) who love to preach at workers and think they know all the answers. Most of them have never organized a strike or bargained a contract, but they think they have the correct position on everything. They love the idea of class struggle unionism but are an obstacle to making it happen.

Writing this book I read a lot of pamphlets put out by the radical campus and antiwar activists who entered the labor movement in the 1970s. Many of them made me cringe. Filled with left-wing jargon, attacking other groups, self-righteous and sectarian, they were the opposite of trying to integrate with the working class and build a socialist movement. Many of these folks spent only a year or two in the working class but had no problem lecturing longtime trade unionists. Although many did good work and they had a class struggle approach, they set back left labor work for decades. Many of the ex-leftists who remained active in the labor movement in the 1980s and beyond recoiled against their youthful 1970s excesses. In doing so, many overcorrected, however, and essentially abandoned class struggle unionism. To be clear, the overall approach of trying to build class struggle unionism was correct, but the know-it-all attitude and disconnect from reality of certain groups was a problem. It was a form of middle-class intellectualism rather than an attempt to fit into a working-class movement.

The goal is to spread class struggle ideas throughout the labor movement, not isolate ourselves as the only true unionists. Even today some leftists believe that being the militant minority means putting out leaflets or, even easier, going on Facebook to denounce the union leadership as sellouts and every union leader as a bureaucrat. To these folks every contract sucks and every strike is a great defeat. They exist only in the world of ideas and as such can always be right.

When a union engages in a militant strike, these armchair leftists invariably criticize the settlement. All contracts include compromise, even strikes. For that reason, strike settlements cannot simply be judged by their terms but on the process used to get there. Did we fight for all that could be won? Did we put management to the test? Did we win all that could be won in the course of the struggle? A lot of armchair quarterbacks who have never been involved in actual workers' struggles like to pick apart strike settlements. Lifelong revolutionary unionist Elizabeth Gurley Flynn, who in her younger IWW days was known as the rebel girl, noted, "What is a labor victory? I maintain it is a twofold thing. Workers must gain economic advantage, but they must also gain revolutionary spirit, in order to achieve a complete victory. For workers to gain a few more cents a day, a few minutes less a day, and go back to work with the same psychology, the same attitude towards society is to have achieved a temporary gain and not a lasting victory."[16]

To Flynn, the effect on the consciousness of the workers is what matters. But to the know-it-alls, a labor victory is what they decide from behind the comfort of their computer screens.

Another danger is believing that your tiny group has all the answers and refusing to work with other groups. As Max Elbaum notes about the 1970s groups utilizing the militant minority approach, "Skilled organizers utilizing this approach could often draw around themselves a small nucleus of left-leaning workers. But it did not encourage the formation of alliances with noncommunist reform leaders (or even with cadre of other communist groups), nor did it give much priority to patient work with rank-and-file workers who were not already radicals."[17]

Folks using this concept have an easy answer to who is the militant minority: they are.

The problem with this approach is the militant minority became little more than an extension of the left-wing groups. As Elbaum writes, "Still, the dominant tendency in the early 1970s saw the key to building 'class struggle unions' as developing opposition caucuses in which communist cadre largely determined the caucus' program and held dominant organizational influence."[18] This is not to say don't build left-wing caucuses—in fact, we do far too little of that. But in doing so, we need a big-tent approach along with a bit of humility. If you believe in class struggle unionism, you work with people where they're at and help move the struggle forward.

Part of this means that class struggle unionists do not need to agree on all points. In fact, there are significant differences among class struggle unionists on key questions. That's OK. Next we will have a discussion of some of these issues that typically have prompted debates among class struggle unionists.

Getting Better Leaders

One of the questions class struggle unionists have confronted is how much effort to place into running union reform efforts. Under this formula, activists gather a group of workers together, establish a reform caucus, critique the union leadership, and eventually run a slate for office. Many labor unions are led by lazy, incompetent leaders who have no plan or vision to transform unions.

Even in its weakened state, the labor movement includes millions of workers, and local and national unions have resources that could be used to take on employers. Having control of the resources of the union would give the platform to implement class struggle policies. For these reasons, getting new leaders is a necessary step in moving the struggle forward.

But while new union leadership is necessary, in and of itself it will not put unions on a class struggle basis. In the absence of a class struggle program and movement, any new leaders elected face the exact same problems as those they replaced. Electing new leaders does not resolve the structural issues of the divide between union staff or officers whose daily existence differs from frontline workers, the constant pressure to compromise inherent in the bureaucratized labor-relations system, and the fundamental weakness of unions today.

There are countless examples of reformers getting in office and, over time, becoming much like those bureaucrats they sought to replace. As one syndicalist leader complained in the 1920s, "Every time we succeeded in making one of our own comrades an official of the trades unions, it turned out that then, instead of a change of tactics taking place, the trades unions corrupted our own comrades too."[19] Without a transformative plan to take on capital on a larger scale, unions are stuck, faced with the same demands for concessions and employer power as those they replaced.

One of the great reform movements of the 1970s was the Miners for Democracy movement, which sought to restore the United Mine Workers of America to a fighting union. After mineworker dissident Jock Yablonski was murdered in his bed by goons hired by UMWA president Tony Boyle, a broad-based reform movement succeeded in getting reformer Arnold Miller elected. Yet in a few short years, Miller came under fire for dictatorial manners and driving a union-provided Cadillac.[20]

Although union reform sounds radical, it is actually a fairly conservative approach because it is essentially saying the problem is just bad leaders. Saying the problem is one of bad leadership minimizes the challenge. For that reason, union reform must be coupled with the other elements of class struggle unionism, most importantly a plan to put unions on a class struggle basis.

One time-honored method is to put forward a class struggle program, organize the workers around the issues, and bring the workers into conflict with the boss. Kim Moody, in his article "The Rank and File Strategy," explains how this strategy was used by the Trotskyist leadership of the 1934 truckers' strike. Moody quotes 1934 strike veteran Farrell Dobbs, explaining, "'Thus, the indicated tactic was to aim the workers' fire straight at the employers and catch the union bureaucrats in the middle.'"[21] Fighting the boss places demands upon the employer that end up isolating and exposing the union leadership who don't want to fight. Union leadership are caught in the crossfire between the demands of the workers and leadership's desire to cooperate with employers.

As Steve Early sums up, "The most successful rank-and-file movements of the long 1970s (and beyond) rooted themselves in the workplace and tried to unite members in contract campaigns and day-to-day fights against the boss, while also attempting to gain control over union structures so the latter could facilitate rather than impede rank-and-file struggles."[22] An example of this approach is the decades-long battle of the Teamsters for a Democratic Union. For decades, TDU has been a major player in contract ratifications, putting out contract bulletins and weighing in on major national contracts. The strategy allows them to expand their reach and actually gain more influence within the union.

This approach has many advantages. First, it focuses on building struggles at the rank-and-file level. Second, it provides a guideline for relating to union officials, which is to work with those who will work with you. Third, it exposes the class traitors, eventually leading to a change in leadership. Finally, it builds up a class struggle union from the shop floor. Rather than talking simply about union internal affairs that many workers may not care about, they end up playing a big role in explaining, and often opposing, contract provisions that workers typically are concerned about.

A classic example of the approach is the rise of the Chicago Teachers Union. A core of activists got together and formed the Caucus of Rank and File Educators. They became the militant minority in their local, uniting with community groups and engaging in fights against school closings.

Based on action, they pulled together a group of teachers who wanted to fight and swept the elections of the Chicago Teachers Union. The rest is history, with their 2012 strike serving as the inspiration for a wave of teacher activism and strikes that continue to this day. This successful strike spurred other strikes, but even more importantly it served as the basis for building a militant minority among teacher activists nationally. This helped spur others to action, leading to an organized grouping within the teachers union, which has led to a strike wave. According to some estimates, over 5 percent of teachers struck in the first half of 2018 alone.[23]

This wave transformed teacher unionism in a way mere electoral reforms could not have accomplished. It pointed the way forward with a program based on militancy, broad educational demands, and strike activity. The teachers coalesced into a national movement that has shared experiences to create a new form of teacher unionism with an agenda of fighting privatization, demanding funding, strike activity, broad social demands, and open participatory bargaining.

Creating New Organizations
versus Transforming Existing Unions

Most unions are bureaucratic, timid, and even corrupt. That has led some to argue that class struggle unionists should not work within the preexisting workers' movement but instead attempt to create new unions that are purer or more left wing. Whereas a generation ago forming alternative unions required a clean break from the AFL-CIO, which was hostile to what it regarded as dual unionism (that is, attempts to set up unions or organizations not officially sanctioned by the labor federation), today the AFL-CIO not only tolerates independent unions and organizations, but it also encourages their formation. But the underlying question remains the same—should class struggle unionists attempt to reform the existing labor movement or build a new one?

In the early 1900s, with the AFL refusing to organize the masses of industrial workers, workers in unskilled positions wanted to fight but simply could not do that through the exclusionary AFL locals. Some of the great strikes in labor history came out of this upsurge, with the IWW providing important leadership. Long after the IWW waned, their influence remained in the battles of the 1930s. A full assessment of the IWW is beyond the scope of this book, although it is one of the great examples of a class struggle approach in US labor history.

William Z. Foster, who was an early member of the IWW, argued that unions should bore from within to take over the AFL. Basing his strategy on the French syndicalists, Foster argued that if leftists abandoned the main labor federations, they merely strengthened the conservatives within them and left the labor movement in reactionary hands. Foster claimed that the weakness of the labor movement in the United States was due to the strategy of dual unionism.

Big Bill Haywood, a leading figure in the IWW who came out of the western mines, scoffed at Foster's argument that the AFL could be reformed:

> *Within craft unions we are told to bore;*
> *To form an apple from a rotten core;*
> *Yet boring till we find ourselves outside;*
> *We will have built a hole—but nothing more.*[24]

To Haywood and others of his day, the AFL was unreformable. This view was the popular view among the left wing of labor, including IWW activists, until the early 1920s, when most class struggle unionists moved toward building struggle within the reactionary AFL unions.

We certainly don't need to resolve historical arguments here. In general, there are pros and cons to any approach. One of the positives of building new organizations is that some unions are so tightly controlled and bureaucratic it is hard to see how they can change. In today's context, isolated from the mainstream of the labor movement, unions are unlikely to be able to deploy the type of militancy needed to revive the labor movement.

But that being said, labor militants should think long and hard about abandoning the labor movement in favor of pure left-wing unions or organizations. Unions have resources and the ability to organize on a grand scale. Historically left-wing unions isolated from the labor movement have been more exposed to government repression. The Communist Party engaged in better strikes of textile workers in Passaic, New Jersey, in 1927 and Gastonia, North Carolina, in 1929. The strikes were bitterly repressed and the strike leadership red-baited. The AFL offered no support and actively undermined the strikes. And if the left unions don't actually organize workers, they can end up more as propaganda sects than real unions.

Ultimately the question must always be, where are the workers in motion or where can they be in motion? If workers are flocking to conservative unions, those who stay in pure left-wing unions can end up isolating themselves from the workers' struggle and abandon the workers to conservative leaders who are unwilling to fight management. In his study on the rise of the International Longshore and Warehouse Union (ILWU), Howard Kimeldorf notes that left-wing leader Harry Bridges and the left had to buck the national Communist Party, who at the time wanted them to continue operating a dual union. The activists resisted the advice, even throwing a party official who came to lay down the law out the window. By working within the decrepit AFL local, Bridges and his fellow militants were able to conduct the general strike in Seattle and go on to found the ILWU, which even today is one of our best unions.[25]

Today, we will likely need a multipronged approach. Those who say militants should work only in existing unions are locking themselves into a weak and declining labor movement where opportunities for militancy may be limited. Yet workers' centers and many alternative or independent unions lack the resources and membership of the existing labor movement. The task has to be to couple the influence of the existing labor movement along with the independence of alternative unionism.

Workers' Centers

Any discussion today of alternative unionism must take into account the pros and cons of the workers' center movement. Today there are over one hundred workers' centers around the country, with over tens of millions of dollars in funding each year. Although a fraction of the size of the labor movement, they have outsized influence on union strategy. Just as we critique unions based on class struggle standards, workers' centers require a similar analysis.

Any analysis of workers' centers must start with funding. Workers' centers are not funded by workers but in large part by billionaire-created foundations. The US Chamber of Commerce estimates that billionaire foundations gave over a hundred million dollars during a three-year period (2013–2016) to workers' centers, leading the chamber to conclude the workers' center movement was "less an autonomous, self-generating phenomenon than it was a creature of the progressive foundations that encouraged and supported it."[26] An independent study by law professors estimates that the major funding sources of workers' centers are "external to the organization (foundation grants, government grants, and individual donations) rather than funding streams that are internally generated, such as membership."[27] The authors estimate that workers' centers get only 1.8 percent of their funding from membership dues.

Let's be crystal clear. A militant, worker-led movement must be funded by workers. As one book written by a grassroots activist collective stated, "The revolution will not be funded."[28] There is a long history of foundations using their money to direct social movements. One of the key points of utilizing workers' centers as opposed to existing unions should be to promote militancy outside the straitjackets of labor law. The billionaire class–funded foundations simply will not allow that to happen.

The union movement is an organic form of worker organization that has repeatedly developed in countries around the world since the rise of capitalism. It comes from workers and the working class. The workers' center movement is different in that it originates largely outside the working class and is not self-sustaining. For that reason, it can never replace the labor movement.

For all of our problems, our labor movement is based on worker self-governance. Even the most corrupt union still must hold elections even if the scales are tilted toward incumbents and staff. Workers' centers face no such accountability. Structurally they are set up as nonprofits, with legal control of the organization residing not in an elected organization of workers but in a board of directors that selects itself. According to one analysis,

> Unlike unions, nonprofit organizations that are organized as membership organizations do not have to give members the right to elect the leadership or to participate in meetings of the organization, except insofar as the organization has adopted by-laws granting such rights. . . . The law governing other mutual benefit membership organizations (professional associations, sports leagues, neighborhood and condominium associations, and so forth) varies from state to state and has considerably less to say about the rights of members in the organization than do the LMRDA and the National Labor Relations Act (NLRA).[29]

Unions have elaborate procedures to decide whether to strike or to authorize picket lines. After all, the union members are losing pay or risking jobs with strike actions. But some workers' centers think nothing of calling for strikes and boycotts of entire industries, such as the 2019 Uber strike, with no vote of the members whose paychecks will be affected. It is a fundamental principle of unionism that workers decide for themselves if they are to strike.

None of this is to say class struggle unionists should not work within workers' centers or that these centers do not perform good work. Many do excellent work. The reason we have a workers' center movement is because of the weakness of the labor movement. With most unions stuck within the business union / labor liberal framework, workers' centers address a need for workers who are not being represented by traditional unions.

There is a wide variety in approaches of workers' centers. On the one extreme we have the Restaurant Opportunities Centers (ROC) United, which has a board of directors composed of heads of non-profits but not one restaurant worker.[30] Programs include training and lobbying efforts but little evidence of shop floor organization. While this may or may not be good social work, it bears little resemblance to worker self-organization or unionism.

As one former restaurant worker who worked for ROC explained on the website Organizing Work, the job didn't provide him the opportunity to fight for workers like he thought it would:

> It took four long years before I came to the realization that I wasn't going to do that working at ROC. Despite their glossy brochures, big budgets, staffers and other resources, I now believe that non-profits are a dead end for social movements and for aspiring organizers. It wasn't until I quit my job at ROC and decided to organize directly with my coworkers at a small restaurant that I really began to grasp what real worker power could look like.[31]

The organization focused on certifying restaurants as model employers and operating training centers to train workers. These may be worthwhile endeavors, but they have little to do with supporting organizing of restaurant workers.

In contrast, the Awood Center in Minneapolis has a strong base among Somali workers at an Amazon distribution center in the Minneapolis suburb of Shakopee.[32] They have been able to conduct several

strikes on particular shifts with solid participation and win concessions from the employers. Some workers' centers such as Chicago
Community and Workers' Rights work to ensure the center's board of
directors is composed of a majority of workers. While all workers' centers must deal with the issue of outside funding, some quite consciously break out of the liberal mode and fight for worker-led activism.

For that reason, it is not possible to conduct a one-size-fits-all
critique of workers' centers. Just as we critiqued the existing labor
movement, each workers' center needs to be analyzed according to
class struggle ideas. In looking at particular centers, we must apply
the same standards we apply to unions:

- Does the center promote sharp class struggle or class collaboration? Tactically does it favor strikes and marches on
  the boss, or does it merely favor legislation, training, or legal service?
- Who controls the organization? Is the board of directors
  composed of workers or staff/outsiders? Who sets the overall strategy? How does funding impact strategy? Are workers props, or do they actually set strategy?
- Are actions rooted in the workplace? Are strikes open-ended
  and democratically controlled by workers, or are they publicity strikes? Does the center have an independent shop floor
  organization?
- Could the center exist without staff and foundation funding? How does funding impact priorities?
- Does the center fit comfortably within the system or is it
  confrontational? Or is the agenda, whether open or hidden,
  merely to pass legislation? Does the center make politicians
  and funders uncomfortable, or is it a darling of the liberal
  elite? Would the center violate injunctions?

Applying these standards, we can avoid a one-size-fits-all critique of workers' centers. We need independent, militant worker
organizations to wage class struggle. So workers' centers could play
a vital role in that. It's not that workers' centers cannot pose a challenge to capital. It's that many don't. That does not mean writing off

workers' centers, but rather, just as with unions, it is our task to put them on a class struggle basis.

Rank-and-File versus Staff Jobs

Socialist groups face a fundamental problem. Although they believe workers should run the economy and the government, the current membership of these socialist groups is not always reflective of that fact. So in order to transform their membership composition they need to organize in the working class. Additionally, believing in class struggle, socialists understand the importance of unions. Strictly speaking, this is not really an issue of trade union strategy but will be important to many who want to orient toward the labor movement.

The question becomes, do folks take a job as a rank-and-file member or as staff? Many college-educated activists such as nurses and teachers are already employed in skilled working-class positions. But activists in other groups wanting to do labor work must decide whether to take a staff job or a job in a workplace.

It is important to realize that this problem is one that exists for a particular group·at a particular point in time. The Communist Party had many working-class union members in the 1930s. According to historian Roger Keeran, "The leading Communists in the automobile industry were workers and unionists of long standing," and Keeran gives an example of a leading autoworker and communist, Wyndham Mortimer, who was a mineworker at age twelve, and "by 1936 Mortimer had been a worker for 40 years and an auto worker for 20 years."[33] Bob Travis, another top party activist and auto leader, "quit school at the age of 16 to work in a forge. By 1936 he had been an autoworker for a dozen years."[34] But the socialist movement today is overwhelmingly based in the middle class.

There are a number of compelling reasons folks should start out in the workplace. Some are quite practical. Implementing a class struggle approach requires independence from the labor officials. The reality is, if you work as a staffer for a union, then the union controls your paycheck, and there are limitations on what you can do. Being a rank-and-file union member gives you lots of freedom to implement a class struggle union approach.

But on a deeper level, how can you be a union leader if you have never been a worker? Just because you get a job as an organizer for the labor movement doesn't mean you're a unionist. Class struggle unionists believe in integrating with the workers and that the working class should be in control. Those who have never worked a real job don't know the oppression of reporting to some dumbshit supervisor or following stupid work rules.

Additionally, we have discussed organizing new industries or transforming existing unions. This all requires rank-and-file organizing and very well could put one at odds with union leadership. Part of having a class struggle approach to organizing is doing things differently. Just being good and efficient union staffers is not going to revive the labor movement.

That said, college-educated activists going into the workplace should not romanticize the process. Thousands went into workplaces in the 1970s, but relatively few stayed. As many of the left-wing groups dissolved in the late 1970s, many drifted into graduate school or took or were elected to staff jobs. Unfortunately, not a lot is written about this period, especially by those who stayed.

Nor should we believe that taking a rank-and-file job in and of itself resolves the issues. Those who take rank-and-file jobs face some of the same constraints that staffers and elected officials face. In the absence of a broader militant-minority approach, the rank-and-file work can end up narrowly focused on workplace issues. In the absence of a class struggle program, this can be depoliticizing.

Another issue we face is that the labor movement is very staff driven. Control over resources in the labor movement often requires holding either an elected position or a staff position. While one can build struggle in one workplace as a rank-and-filer, in order to build a labor movement capable of confronting capital requires a broader perspective and influence, which is often concentrated in these staff positions. For that reason, many activists, even those who start out in the workplace, may find themselves in a full-time elected or staff role. Regardless, maintaining the principles of class struggle unionism, particularly the points on workers' self-representation, is critical to keeping your bearings in these situations.

It's best to view both the rank-and-file strategy and militant minority as subsets of an overall class union strategy. Any union strategy must offer guidance to folks at all positions within the union movement. The overall strategy is to put unionism on a class struggle basis utilizing class struggle ideas and tactics. To do so requires both a rank-and-file orientation and utilization of the militant-minority method.

Beyond Trade Unionism

Trade unionism in and of itself can never solve our problems. Unions can win higher wages, can fight for more shop floor power, and can provide a basis for working-class organization in society. Unionism, in and of itself, cannot eliminate the billionaire class or eliminate exploitation in the workplace. Class struggle unionists see unionism as important but as part and parcel of a larger struggle against exploitation. For that reason, many class struggle unionists combine their trade union work with socialist political work.

We need to be clear. The point of unionism is to fight for better conditions for the working class—not to overthrow the capitalist system. Discussing broader theories is out of the scope of this book. Class struggle unionists do not need to agree on these larger political questions. It is our belief in the illegitimacy of the employment transactions that both unites us and leads to a stronger unionism. But we should at least understand what we are up against.

A 2019 article in the *New York Times* made an argument not typically found in an establishment paper: "Billionaires should not exist—at least not in their present numbers, with their current globe-swallowing power, garnering this level of adulation, while the rest of the economy scrapes by."[35] As the author notes, once you reach a certain level of wealth, it no longer makes sense. The extreme wealth "buys political power, it silences dissent, it serves primarily to perpetuate ever-greater wealth, often unrelated to any reciprocal social good." Now, that the *New York Times*, an establishment paper not known for taking radical positions, espouses such views is a sign of our times and an indication of how out of whack things have become.

While millions of Americans suffered job losses and economic insecurity during the 2020 coronavirus pandemic, the billionaire class saw their wealth skyrocket, jumping $434 billion, or 15 percent, in only two months.[36] In 2020, there were 633 billionaires in the United States, and the minimum wealth on the Forbes 400 list was $2.1 billion.[37] The total combined wealth of the 2020 Forbes 400 list was $3.2 trillion.

That's a lot of money, although the scale of a billion dollars is hard to grasp. Half of the people in the US don't have $400 in their bank accounts to cover emergencies. To get a sense of the scale, 400 seconds would be 6 minutes and 40 seconds. A billion seconds is 32 years. Now, the mythology is this incredible wealth somehow rewards their hard work, special skills, or innovation. But the amount is far beyond what could ever be considered compensation for work. If one was paid $5,000 a day for every single day since Columbus stumbled upon America in 1492, one would still not have a billion dollars.

Even the most militant unionism in and of itself does not disturb these power relationships or even substantially diminish the billionaire class. That's why in addition to unionism, many class struggle unionists engage in socialist political activism to diminish or abolish the control of the billionaire class over our society.

At some level, negotiating a labor contract is bargaining over the terms of our exploitation. By agreeing to even the best union contract, we are agreeing to a situation where the billionaire class gets richer off our labor. As British labor commentator Perry Anderson noted back in the late 1960s, "As institutions, unions do not *challenge* the existence of society based on a division of classes, they merely *express* it."[38] As Anderson explained, the very existence of labor agreements accepts the billionaires' control of society. Unions "both resist the given unequal distribution of income within the society by their wage demands, and ratify the principle of an unequal distribution by their existence."[39] Either explicitly or implicitly the very fact of a contract ties us to an unequal system.

The early AFL leaders such as Samuel Gompers and AFL secretary Peter McGuire, founder of the United Brotherhood of Carpenters and Joiners of America, were socialists who believed that mere unionism would bring about socialism as a gradual process. Indeed for much of union history, a good portion of labor activists agreed with some form of socialist political theory. The early union constitutions placed union struggles within the struggle between the oppressors and the oppressed.

Some of the more radical unionists of Gompers's time came to believe that the labor movement activity could supplant capitalism but that it would take a bitter struggle including general strikes. This branch of unionism, known as revolutionary syndicalism, saw the union movement as a step toward a new society. According to Perry Anderson, "The belief that the trade unions were the chosen instruments for achieving socialism was the main tenet of syndicalism, the revolutionary version of exclusive reliance on trade unions. For this tradition . . . the general strike was the weapon which would abolish capitalist society."[40] The difficulty with that viewpoint is most unionists don't start out holding these revolutionary views. Workers join unions to solve immediate problems. Revolutionary unions face a difficulty that in nonrevolutionary times their unions would not necessarily be the instruments of revolution but rather would have to make accommodations with capital.

But even if unions don't bring about social revolution, they play an important part in furthering solidarity and class consciousness. Back in the early 1900s, intense class conflict bordering on warfare led the Western Federation of Miners to embrace revolutionary unionism. According to Melvyn Dubofsky, "Ten years of industrial violence led such men to move from 'pure and simple' unionism to industrial unionism to socialism and finally to syndicalism."[41]

For that reason, Marxist thinkers have long viewed strikes as important in building class consciousness and moving toward socialism.

Anyone who has gone through a strike knows what I mean. Workers develop solidarity on the picket line; they learn who their friends and enemies are, and the role of government and media is laid bare. The root of this lies in the unnatural order created by the employment relationship under capitalism. We live in a society where we are supposed to be free people with constitutional rights and individual liberty (at least in theory and differentially distributed). But when you enter the workplace you are treated like shit. A strike, however, breaks these unnatural bonds. Ask any striker or unionist—the first days on a picket line are exhilarating.

Today the billionaire class is destroying the planet, impoverishing millions, stealing our pensions and our futures. They will never stop hating us—we are locked in a battle to the death. Class struggle unionism is the one force in society that has the capacity to pull tens of millions into sharp struggle with the billionaires.

Chapter 7

Class Struggle Strategy

In previous chapters we discussed how our leading ideas, our tactics, and our organizing approach should all flow from our understanding of the class struggle between the working class and the billionaire class. The same is true for questions of overall strategy, meaning our program to revive the labor movement. This must also flow from our understanding of the conflict between the working class and the billionaire class.

Business unionists seek modest improvements in particular workplaces. Labor liberals attempt to help disadvantaged workers by operating on their behalf, by doing things *for* them. Class struggle unionists, however, seek to contend with capital on a grand scale, seeking to change the balance of forces between the working class and the billionaire class.

It is always hard when you discuss long-term objectives because the end goal seems so far away. The problem is if we as class struggle unionists don't start redefining our objectives, future unionists will be having the same discussion decades down the road. My first involvement with labor, other than growing up in a union household, was the strike at Hormel in Austin, Minnesota, in 1986, thirty-five years ago. Since then I have seen the labor movement lurch from project to project, none really getting us closer to our objective. If we had continued to concentrate on building a fighting labor movement, we would be a lot closer to our objective.

Over a decade ago, I was writing my first book, *Reviving the*

Strike. Nowadays, it seems most believe the strike is a necessary element of union power. But back then, even in progressive labor circles, I got raised eyes for suggesting the revival of the strike was a matter of critical importance. Here, a similar logic is at play. This time, however, our issue is bigger—changing how we approach unionism.

The reason laying out long-term objectives is important is because it helps give guidance to our short-term work. Day to day, we are not organizing entire industries or developing grand strategic approaches—you may be a member of a public-worker local or a shop steward at UPS dealing with grievances. But our day-to-day unionism should fit within a broader framework and objective. What sort of labor movement are we building? What demands are we putting on union officials? Those questions cannot be answered without an overall class struggle strategy.

Not surprisingly, in developing a strategy we need to break with both labor liberalism and business unionism. Labor liberals are not primarily interested in reorganizing industries or confronting capital. They seek publicity to influence progressive legislation. In the past several decades we have seen high-profile campaigns at the least densely organized sectors of the US economy, including those that have proven difficult to organize. SEIU spent well north of a hundred million dollars organizing fast-food workers over the last decade without organizing a single bargaining unit or creating any self-sustaining organization. Likewise, the United Food and Commercial Workers (UFCW) spent millions on a campaign of largely public relations efforts targeting Walmart, with little to show.

Now, no one would deny that fast-food workers need a union, but by traditional union standards this is one of the harder industries to organize. It's a low-wage job, franchisees are the employers, and there's lots of turnover. If one was planning an assault on corporate power, it is hard to see an argument that this would be *the* key industry to start with. But as we discussed earlier, labor liberals use workplace campaigns as a springboard for legislative action, rather than as a means of organizing workers in an industry into unions.

The UFCW spent millions of dollars attempting to organize Walmart workers in 2012–2015. Retired organizing director at the ILWU Peter Olney responded with an article titled "Where Did the OUR Walmart Campaign Go Wrong?" in which he analyzes the campaign's entire strategic focus rather than organizing mistakes.[1] Olney notes that OUR Walmart chose not to organize the strategic warehouse workers, focusing instead on the retail side, where it was able to get fewer than one hundred workers to strike in their so-called nationwide strikes out of a workforce of over one hundred thousand. But on a deeper level, the OUR Walmart initiative targeted one of the largest employers in the country rather than going after easier targets such as regional non-union grocery chains.

Likewise, labor liberals are fixated on the gig economy. Now, this is nothing new—for decades middle-class liberals have been declaring that jobs are disappearing due to automation and converted in casual employment. But a 2019 report by the Economic Policy Institute found that

> in spite of the rising popularity of service apps like Uber, workers were slightly more likely to have standard work arrangements in 2017 than in 2005. Specifically, in May 2017, the total share of the labor force working in nonstandard work arrangements was 10.1 percent, down from 10.9 percent in 2005. That means nine out of 10 workers were employed in a standard work arrangement in their main job—and this proportion has been relatively stable since 1995.[2]

This definition of nonstandard work includes independent contractors, day laborers, on-call workers, and temp agencies. So 90 percent of workers work for a standard employer. The gig portion, which includes electronic platforms such as Uber and TaskRabbit, was much smaller, with only 1 percent of workers participating in either a first or second job.

Finally, in terms of our strategic focus, there is a significant trend within the progressive wing of labor that views our problems as primarily a lack of correct organizing skills or techniques as opposed to a class struggle strategy capable of taking on capital. This has led to a focus on small employers, particularly the Industrial Workers of the World. While this has the advantage of testing out new strategies in workplaces that are more manageable especially for a union without resources, this does not represent a strategic plan to take on capital. While experimentation has its value, it is time for class struggle unionists to pool our resources to reorganize the industries at the heart of the US economy.

Building Class Struggle Tactics

If we want a fighting labor movement, we need to fight. In some ways, it is as simple as that. So while a lot of this book is about big ideas, the core of it is picking fights with the billionaire class.

Putting the entire labor movement on a class struggle basis seems like a daunting task. So another way of thinking about it is, what type of workers' movement would it take to blockade workplaces, violate injunctions, and engage in outlawed solidarity tactics? How can we pick some battles and move them beyond the existing system? Can this be done in existing unions or will it require new ones, or a combination of both?

This produces a more manageable set of tasks. The question becomes, what would it take to employ class struggle tactics in your industry or to organize a new industry? In all likelihood it would take a core of workers, grassroots organization, and a set of ideas validating this activism. It would need to be pretty radical, a lot more so than existing efforts. While it may take independent worker organization, they would not likely be attractive to the billionaire-funded foundations.

The beauty is, the very tactics necessary for class struggle unionism are the tactics that create militant consciousness. There is nothing like being on a picket line up against the National Guard and seeing the corporate media show their true colors to clarify class lines. The statewide strikes, illegal conflicts with the existing order, and widespread strikes all create a true class movement. Militancy also quickly reveals who are friends and enemies within the labor movement. So in many ways, the development of a class struggle trend will not be separated from the development of militancy.

In a 2020 article in Labor Notes, Mark Meinster, an international rep for United Electrical Workers and longtime class struggle unionist, argues that for the labor movement to revive will require a working-class upsurge. Meinster notes three elements in helping make that happen: 1) more strike activity, 2) workplace militants, and 3) independent organization.[3] By breaking up the overall objective into pieces, we can start building the type of labor movement we need.

Part of this requires revisiting chapter 5, Class Struggle Tactics. When folks say it can't be done, they are really saying we can't reorganize industries within the confines of the current system. They are right. But the real question is, can we envision creating a labor movement capable of violating labor law? We cannot revive the labor movement without violating labor law.

So what are the short-term and intermediate steps of building a labor movement capable of violating labor law? It would seem we need a number of things:

- Popularize class struggle ideas that justify breaking labor law.
- Break with the philosophy of making due within the existing system.
- Discuss what sort of institutions we need to withstand injunctions.
- Understand which issues would get large numbers of workers in motion.
- Pick fights based on class struggle tactics.

Every step we take toward fighting the billionaires helps build a class struggle labor movement.

Building a Class Struggle Trend

As organizers, if we want a class struggle trend within the labor movement, we need to build it. That means pulling together like-minded people, organizing around the issues, and so on. It is about creating a space for discussions on these bigger questions.

Clearly there are many folks in the labor movement who see themselves as class struggle unionists. Some are veterans of the 1970s Marxist movement, others are members of various socialist groups, and some are independent workers who subscribe to these views. Others are militant trade unionists who understand class struggle. But in terms of class struggle unionism as a cohesive trend, we're probably at the lowest point of cohesion in over a hundred years.

Now, the biggest grouping of folks in the labor movement for a number of years has been Labor Notes. Labor Notes was founded by class struggle unionists and today pulls together militant trade unionists through its biannual conference and regional training events. Labor Notes is an important gathering place and is true to its slogan of putting the *movement* back in the labor movement. It is a reflection of the broader labor movement and as such reflects a mixture of social unionism, class struggle unionism, union reform, and an approach that favors organizing skills. It is an important vehicle for class struggle unionists looking to share struggles and tactics.

Overall, the state of the reform movement is weak compared to historical standards. The largest reform caucus is within the Teamsters union, anchored by the decades-old Teamsters for a Democratic Union (TDU). The success of TDU shows the importance and value of building enduring institutions for rank-and-file power. But in other unions, even those with a strong history of reform movements, there is relative quiet.

Beyond that, the greatest strength for the reform movement is the teacher reform movement. Spurred by the Chicago Teachers Union that carried out strikes in 2012 and 2019, the teacher reform movement has spread to other cities. Rather than just offering a change of leadership, Chicago Teachers Union offers a class struggle approach to the crisis in teacher unionism. The elements include a break with pro-corporate Democrats who have participated in defunding and privatizing public education for decades, a militant rank-and-file approach that includes strike activity, and the adoption of broad class-based bargaining demands.

What then does it mean to build a trend or a tendency? In the years leading up to the 1930s, a very broad trend agitated for industrial unionism. This included folks who disagreed on many questions such as the IWW, the Communist Party, and reform-minded bureaucrats at AFL conventions. Likewise, in the 1980s, many left-wing trade unionists came together in a broad anti-concessions movement.

In some ways we can look at the movement of the social unionists over the last couple of decades. Now, in a sense, they have it easier because they can attract foundation funding and support of union officials because their program does not challenge the status quo. But they have put out a conscious line and even organized conferences. They explicitly advance a approach to labor's crisis.

The absence of such a class struggle trend impacts our work more than we know. Without such a trend, it is hard to hold national officials accountable. How can we get national officials to believe in re-organizing industries when even *we* don't believe it is possible? If we think the problem is simply one of organizing strategies, we will put no demands on the leadership of our unions. In the last chapter, we discussed how the core of building the militant-minority strategy in a local or industry involved putting out a program for revitalization.

Among the international unions, the United Electrical Workers still holds to a class struggle perspective. One of the eleven left-led unions, UE was driven out of the AFL in the 1950s and saw its once half a million membership relentlessly raided by pro-company unions. Nonetheless, UE remains true to its beliefs and in 2020 published a pamphlet of UE principles that parallels many of the ideas in this book. The pamphlet lays out many of the key elements of class struggle unionism and calls for a different type of labor movement, which it calls "Them and Us Unionism":

> For the past several decades labor leaders and academics have proposed a wide variety of strategies to rebuild the U.S. labor movement: from better communications work, to giving more money to politicians, to restructuring of the labor movement and its federations, to investments in staff-driven organizing efforts.

But none of it has worked, because none of those strategies recognize that the core issue facing unions, today and throughout history, is the fundamental difference of interests between workers and employers in the capitalist system. . . .

The labor movement we need must be a militant movement, built from the bottom up, and it must be based on clear-cut principles: aggressive struggle, rank and file control, political independence, international solidarity and uniting all workers—in other words, Them and Us Unionism. UE is dedicated to helping achieve that kind of a labor movement.[4]

These ideas should form the basis of discussion of how to revive the labor movement.

Put No Demands, Expect Nothing

Now, some may say our numbers are small within the labor movement and we don't have the power to organize entire industries. That is true. We can come up with all the grand plans to organize industries we want, but how to put it into action?

But this is why class struggle unionists have long put demands upon the labor leadership. With the understanding that our numbers are small, one of our tasks is to influence the course of the labor movement overall. When I started in the labor movement, that approach was very much alive. The remnant of the 1970s left carried out a rank-and-file approach that responded to the union-busting offensive with a rallying cry of "No Concessions." A broad-based movement supported local unions fighting back, who were often undermined by national leadership. In 1983 Jane Slaughter of Labor Notes wrote the book *Concessions and How to Beat Them*, which was both a guide to activists but also a demand upon the national union leadership.

Likewise, when most national unions fell for labor-management cooperation schemes in the early 1990s (and well before that in the auto industry), folks came together to defeat them. Again Labor Notes published books against "Team Concept," the labor-management collaboration schemes popular with union officials at the time. In Minnesota, I was part of a group of trade unionists who formed a group called Meeting the Challenge, drawing hundreds to a conference strategizing about how to defeat these schemes. These efforts both organized workers and put demands upon union leadership.

These initiatives provided organizing tools for rank-and-file workers to fight against concessions and labor-management cooperation. But they also established an ideological pole within the labor movement, challenging key assumptions of business unionism. But over the course of time, and in large part due to the rise of the organizing approach from the labor liberals in the 1990s, the focus of progressives became one of organizing techniques. Rather than wait for the do-nothing bureaucrats, organizers would rebuild the labor movement through their talents and techniques.

There are a number of problems with this approach. First, it puts no demands upon the leadership of the national unions and turns attention away from the timidness and class collaborationism of the labor movement. The key problems in the labor movement are class collaborationism, the decrepit state of the labor movement, and the failure to confront the repressive labor laws in this country. No amount of organizing training can change that.

But at a deeper level, our problem as a labor movement is not lack of organizing skills, it is the absence of a class struggle strategy capable of confronting capital. Today the labor movement is at its weakest in over one hundred years. Only six in one hundred private-sector workers belong to unions. Those that remain are in legacy industries, often unionized workforces in a non-union sea, struggling to maintain their wages and benefits.

In the years leading up to the 1930s, against all odds, class struggle unionists believed they could reorganize basic industries and take on the capitalist (or billionaire) class. The key strikes of the 1930s were not looked at as mere battles with individual employers but as systematic assaults on the power of capital, attacking key fortresses such as auto, steel, and transport. Unionization was viewed by labor and management alike as industrial warfare. Today, there is no such strategic approach to take on the billionaire class.

Class struggle unionists have long argued that manufacturing and closely related industries such as construction, utilities, and transportation are key industries to unionize. This is not a value choice about the workers involved but because if you think of unionization as part of class struggle, you look at where power comes from in society. In the first chapter of this book, we discussed how the billionaire class gets its power because, although working people produce things of value in society, the billionaires pocket the fruits of workers' labor, day in and day out.

Although many argue America has been deindustrialized, Kim Moody, in his book *On New Terrain*, argues that manufacturing remains an important sector of the American economy. Moody notes that although the percent of workers employed in manufacturing has fallen over the decades, there are still millions of workers involved in production, and many jobs the government classifies as service are in reality manufacturing.

While some of the job loss is due to offshoring, Moody notes that increasing productivity plays a key role, arguing that "a more than doubling of productivity since the early 1980s can well explain much of the 50 percent drop in manufacturing production worker jobs over that long period."[5] But that also means each industrial worker produces more in each workday. The beauty of it is this means striking by these workers hits the employers way harder.

A closely related industry to manufacturing is the area of logistics that involves getting products to stores or increasingly to homes for purchase. Logistics includes transportation and warehousing of goods and plays an increasingly important role in the modern economy. As Joe Allen noted a number of years ago in *Jacobin* magazine, this area is of strategic importance.

> The US economy revolves around the sprawling logistics industry, and the potential power of these workers is enormous. Socialists should always seek a political relationship with those sections of the working class that have the potential power to elevate the organization and politics of the entire class. Without a strong left wing based in the most powerful workplaces, both the

working-class movement and the socialist left will continue to be of marginal influence.[6]

Allen notes that the logistics industry is an integral part of the manufacturing of goods. For that reason, many have discussed this as a potential choke point. One would think this group of strategic, underpaid, geographically concentrated workers would constitute the core of any union strategy. But while tens of millions of dollars are spent on fast-food and retail campaigns, relatively little attention is given to this organizing.

Now, none of this is to say these are the only industries that we need to reorganize. Trucking, meatpacking, construction, and most other industries are virtually non-union. In addition, other key industries have emerged over the last century. The system has a great appetite and seeks to take all of human activity—such as child-rearing, education, food preparation, health care, and more— and turn them into profit-making activities for the billionaire class. As Moody notes, historically, "This was unpaid labor performed by women mostly in the home, though, as we shall see, it has now been partially transformed into commodity production, also performed by women."[7] Of these, health care has transformed into a major source of value for the billionaire class, helping to explain the hostility to national health care.

But despite all of these industries, and hundreds of millions of workers in desperate need of a militant labor movement, most of the national union leadership is missing in action. While the labor liberals are at least trying to do something, the business unionists are completely silent. Whereas thirty years ago there was some sense of crisis, today there is complacency. But even more alarming, those who want a fighting labor movement have quit demanding change.

It was not always like this. In the 1970s and 1980s, the left of the labor movement railed against the establishment, denouncing union sellouts. A vibrant anti-concessions movement sought to hold the line, and unionists joined together to fight the Central Intelligence Agency's domination of AFL-CIO policy. Even into the early 2000s, the New Voice movement demanded changes in the AFL-CIO prior to splitting to form Change to Win, the alternative labor federation that has gone nowhere. But at least there was a sense of crisis, of the idea that we could demand our union leaders do something. The labor movement is in crisis. Yet the AFL-CIO, rather than sponsor conferences or put together a plan to reorganize basic industries, made the focus of their strategic initiative the Commission on the Future of Work and Unions.[8] The commission produced uninspiring insights such as collective bargaining is good and the gains from technology should be shared by workers. It is worth a read if only to see how out of touch and useless the AFL-CIO has become.

The United Auto Workers have no plan to organize the southern auto plants or the parts suppliers. The Teamsters have no plan to organize the now largely non-union trucking industry. The United Food and Commercial Workers have no strategy to organize the 87 percent of meatpacking workers denied union representation or to improve the conditions of their remaining members. The construction unions rely on government contracts and prevailing wage legislation and seek to prove that they add value to a dwindling number of union contractors. The labor movement is in dire straits.

Yet we have largely let them off the hook. For the last generation, for the first time in labor history, those who want a fighting labor movement have quit putting demands upon our leadership. Many young leftists entering the labor movement probably have a dim view of the labor bureaucracy. Seeing the union movement as messed up, they start workers' centers or independent initiatives. Others segregate themselves within organizing departments, convincing themselves they are better than the hacks in the rest of the union. They try to do as much good as they can within the system while maintaining their ideals.

But our task is a lot bigger than that. We need to build a class struggle union movement capable of waging war against an entire class of billionaires with untold political and economic power. It is not enough to be good organizers; we need to demand that the labor movement make the changes necessary to turn into a fighting, militant movement. This entire book has argued that we need class struggle ideology combined with class struggle organizing and class struggle tactics to make gains. Whatever route people take, it's important to proceed based on class struggle principles, otherwise we end up with reformist organizations after all that effort.

Conclusion

I have been doing labor work for more than three decades. I have sat in countless bargaining sessions, fought grievances, done arbitrations, approached workers about joining unions, worked on strikes, and held countless contract ratification meetings. I have closely followed the labor commentary over the last several decades and contributed to the debate.

I believe the labor movement is adrift. We have no plan, no prospects, and most importantly have not really come to grips that we are lost. But it does not need to be that way. We need to free ourselves from the practical and ideological straitjacket that has been imposed on us and our unionism.

We are up against a ruthless and uncompromising enemy. One which believes every sphere of human activity should enrich them as a class and views our unions as one of the few things that can prevent their domination. The billionaire class views our unions as the enemy, as key institutions of the working class. Like it or not, they are engaged in a class struggle against us.

We have a choice. Are we going to continue on the failed strategies of the last decades, or are we going to adopt a philosophy with a proven ability to confront our enemies? Class struggle unionism is actually quite simple. It grounds all our actions and all our strategies on a simple proposition: that workers create all wealth, and a system that allows the few to obtain billions in riches while the producers of wealth live in misery is an illegitimate system. Once we accept that essential reality and act as a class, victory will be ours.

I am incredibly hopeful. When I started work in the labor

movement, discussion of class issues was taboo. Those who questioned the unjust economic system were marginalized. But a lot has changed in recent decades.

The Occupy movement of 2011 put the 1 percent on the map, introducing the billionaire class to popular discussion. The Black Lives Matter movement has shown the power of working people rising up against oppression. The campaigns of politicians such as Bernie Sanders and Alexandria Ocasio-Cortez inspired millions to challenge a corrupt political system. Mass movements of workers, such as in the Wisconsin uprising and the Chicago and red state teachers' strikes, showed that real change comes from working people getting in motion.

We know from history that real change happens when ordinary working people refuse to accept their conditions. When millions rise up against exploitation and demand a better world. We also know that class struggle unionism is a powerful ideology, one hated and feared by the billionaire class. We have a world to win, and the future is bright.

Acknowledgments

I started my journey in unionism in the 1980s and learned many of my lessons from the bitter class struggle strikes of the 1980s and 1990s. One of the great joys is to see people transform themselves through struggle, and I have seen folks do incredible things over the years when engaged in struggle.

Writing a book on class struggle unionism is an ambitious affair. No one has all the answers. What I have tried to do is capture the best of what I have seen over the last few decades of labor work. Over the years I have worked with many class struggle unionists. The one quality that stands out in these folks, other than tireless work, is their devotion to the working class.

Many unionists gave feedback on the drafts of this book, including Jane Slaughter, Jesse Sharkey, Marianne LeNabat, Luisa M., Gregory Butler, Michael Yates, Ellen David Freedman, Mark Meinster, J. Burger, Cherene Horazuk, Steve Early, and Chris Townsend. Many of the critiques made me reshape my formulations and helped create a better product.

Haymarket editor Ashley Smith supplied valuable and detailed critiques of the concepts in the book, helping sharpen my commentary. Michael Trudeau was the copyeditor and did a great job correcting my writing and citations. His work is much appreciated.

Haymarket Books understands and believes in radical unionism. Julie Fain is a supportive publisher and a delight to work with along with the entire Haymarket team. They perform a valuable service for our class struggle labor movement, and it's great to work with them.

Notes

Chapter 1: Shop Floor Economics

1. Michael Zweig, "Six Points on Class," *Monthly Review* 58, no. 3 (July–August 2006): 117.
2. Kerry Dolan, ed., "The Forbes 400: The Definitive Ranking of the Wealthiest Americans in 2020," *Forbes*, September 8, 2020, www.forbes.com/forbes-400.
3. Michael Yates, *The Great Inequality* (New York: Routledge, 2016), 26.
4. Catherine Clifford, "The Majority of Billionaires in the World Are Self-Made," CNBC, May 10, 2019, www.cnbc.com/2019/05/10/wealthx-billionaire -census-majority-of-worlds-billionaires-self-made.html.
5. Michael Parenti, *Democracy for the Few* (Boston: Wadsworth Cengage Learning, 2008), 7.
6. Heidi Chung, "The Richest 1% Own 50% of Stocks Held by American Households," Yahoo! Finance, January 17, 2019, https://finance .yahoo.com/news/the-richest-1-own-50-of-stocks-held-by-american -households-150758595.html. See also G. William Domhoff, "Power in America: Wealth, Income, and Power," WhoRulesAmerica.net, last modified April 2017, https://whorulesamerica.ucsc.edu/power/wealth.html.
7. Thomas Piketty, *Capital in the Twenty-First Century* (Cambridge, MA: Belknap Press of Harvard University Press, 2017), 547–48, Kindle edition.
8. Arvind Dilawar, "Amazon Is the Best Argument against Capitalism," *Pacific Standard*, February 7, 2019, https://psmag.com/ideas/amazon-is-the-best -argument-against-capitalism.
9. Dilawar, "Amazon Is the Best Argument against Capitalism."
10. Karl Marx and Eleanor Marx Aveling, *Value, Price, and Profit* (Chicago: Charles H. Kerr, 1910), 84.
11. Bill Fletcher and Fernando Gapasin, *Solidarity Divided: The Crisis in Organized Labor and a New Path toward Social Justice* (Berkeley: University of California Press, 2009), 166–67.
12. Michael Yates, *Can the Working Class Change the World?* (New York: Monthly Review Press, 2018), 38.
13. Marx to Pavel Vasilyevich Annenkov, December 28, 1846, in *Marx Engels*

Collected Works, vol. 38 (London: Lawrence & Wishart, 1982), 95.

Chapter 2: Class Struggle Union Ideas

1. Bernie Sanders, "It's Time to Complete the Revolution We Started," *Guardian*, February 25, 2019, www.theguardian.com/commentisfree/2019/feb/25/its-time-to-complete-the-revolution-we-started.
2. Philip Taft, "On the Origins of Business Unionism," *Industrial and Labor Relations Review* 17, no. 1 (October 1963): 20.
3. Robert F. Hoxie, "Trade Unionism in the United States: General Character and Types," *Journal of Political Economy* 22, no. 3 (March 1914): 212.
4. Farrell Dobbs, *Teamster Power* (New York: Monad Press, 1973), 33–34.
5. Melvyn Dubofsky, *"Big Bill" Haywood* (New York: St. Martin's, 1987), 33.
6. James J. Matles and James Higgins, *Them and Us: Struggles of a Rank-and-File Union* (Pittsburgh: United Electrical, Radio and Machine Workers of America, 1995).
7. Frederick Thompson and Patrick Murfin, *The I.W.W.: Its First Seventy Years (1905–1975); The History of an Effort to Organize the Working Class* (Chicago: Industrial Workers of the World, 1976), 9. See also James Weinstein, *The Corporate Ideal in the Liberal State: 1900–1918* (Boston: Beacon Press, 1968), 8.
8. Philip S. Foner, *History of the Labor Movement in the United States*, vol. 9, *The T.U.E.L. to the End of the Gompers Era* (New York: International Publishers, 1991), 184.
9. William Z. Foster, *Misleaders of Labor* (New York: Trade Union Education League, 1927), 43.
10. Mother Jones, *Autobiography of Mother Jones* (Chicago: Charles H. Kerr, 1925), 136.
11. Karl Marx, "General Rules, October 1864," International Workingmen's Association (1864), www.marxists.org/history/international/iwma/documents/1864/rules.htm.
12. Joe Allen, "The Rank and File Strategy: A Resource List," Midwest Socialist, June 7, 2019, https://midwestsocialist.com/2019/06/07/the-rank-and-file-strategy-a-resource-list.
13. Hal Draper, "Why the Working Class Is the Key to Progress," in *Introduction to Independent Socialism*, 2nd ed. (Berkeley, CA: Independent Socialist Press, 1970), 60–64, available at https://www.marxists.org/history/etol/document/is-us/IS-documents/70-72/70-(5).pdf.
14. Yates, *Can the Working Class Change the World?*, 36.
15. Richard Hyman, *The Political Economy of Industrial Relations: Theory and Practice in a Cold Climate* (Basingstoke, UK: Macmillan, 1989), 20–21.
16. David Montgomery, *Workers' Control in America: Studies in the History of Work, Technology, and Labor Struggles*, rev. ed. (Cambridge, UK: Cambridge University Press, 1980), and Montgomery, *The Fall of the House of Labor: The*

Workplace, the State, and American Labor Activism, 1865–1925 (Cambridge, UK: Cambridge University Press, 1987).

17. Micah Uetricht and Barry Eidlin, "US Union Revitalization and the Missing 'Militant Minority,'" *Labor Studies Journal* 44, no. 1 (March 2019): 40, doi.org/10.1177/0160449x19828470.

18. Kim Moody, *On New Terrain: How Capital Is Reshaping the Battleground of Class War* (Chicago: Haymarket Books, 2018), 18.

19. Toni Gilpin, *The Long Deep Grudge: A Story of Big Capital, Radical Labor, and Class War in the American Heartland* (Chicago: Haymarket Books, 2020), 190.

20. Gilpin, *Long Deep Grudge*, 195.

21. Gilpin, *Long Deep Grudge*, 197.

22. Andrew Kolin, *Political Economy of Labor Repression in the United States* (Lanham, MD: Lexington Books, 2018), 204.

23. Kolin, *Political Economy of Labor Repression*, 204.

24. Judith Stepan-Norris and Maurice Zeitlin, *Left Out: Reds and America's Industrial Unions* (Cambridge, UK: Cambridge University Press, 2005), 144.

25. A. C. Jones, "UAW Rank-and-File Opposition during the Long 1970s" in *Rebel Rank and File: Labor Militancy and Revolt from Below in the Long 1970s*, eds. Aaron Brenner, Robert Brenner, and Cal Winslow (London: Verso, 2010), 285.

26. Jones, "UAW Rank-and-File Opposition," 299.

27. Tom Laney, "Interview with Solidarity Unionist Tom Laney," *Solidarity Review*, February 16, 2018, http://web.archive.org/web/20190615082549/ https://www.solidarityreview.com/latestnews/tomlaneyinterview.

28. James B. Atleson, *Values and Assumptions in American Labor Law* (Amherst: University of Massachusetts Press, 1983), 177.

29. Parenti, *Democracy for the Few*, 160.

Chapter 3: Beyond Labor Liberalism

1. Fletcher and Gapasin, *Solidarity Divided*, 61.

2. Stephanie Ross, "Varieties of Social Unionism: Towards a Framework for Comparison," *Just Labour: A Canadian Journal of Work and Society* 11 (Autumn 2007): 17.

3. Zinn Education Project, "Sept. 26, 1909: International Ladies' Garment Workers' Union Strike," www.zinnedproject.org/news/tdih/ILGWU-strike.

4. Andy Stern, *A Country That Works: Getting America Back on Track* (New York: Free Press, 2008), 59.

5. Stern, *Country That Works*, 70.

6. Workers Lab, "2019 Year in Review," January 7, 2020, www.theworkerslab.com /blog/end-of-year-report.

7. Robert Bussel, *From Harvard to the Ranks of Labor: Powers Hapgood and the American Working Class* (University Park: Pennsylvania State University Press, 1999), 56.

8. Len De Caux, *Labor Radical: From the Wobblies to CIO, a Personal History* (Boston: Beacon Press, 1971), 34.
9. Max Elbaum, *Revolution in the Air: Sixties Radicals Turn to Lenin, Mao and Che* (New York: Verso, 2018), 166.
10. Thomas Geoghegan, *Which Side Are You On? Trying to Be for Labor When It's Flat on Its Back* (New York: New Press, 2004), 78.
11. Stern, *Country That Works*, 39.
12. Steve Early, *The Civil Wars in US Labor: Birth of a New Workers' Movement or Death Throes of the Old?* (Chicago: Haymarket Books, 2011), 20.
13. Early, *Civil Wars in US Labor*, 18.
14. Early, *Civil Wars in US Labor*, 109–136.
15. Matthew Dimick, "Labor Rights Will Not Save the Labor Movement," *Jacobin*, December 12, 2019, www.jacobinmag.com/2019/12/labor-rights-movement-freedom-nlra-nlrb-mass-picketing.
16. Dimick, "Labor Rights Will Not Save the Labor Movement."
17. Dimick, "Labor Rights Will Not Save the Labor Movement."

Chapter 4: Class Struggle Unionists Fight for the Entire Working Class

1. "Racial Economic Inequality," Inequality.org, August 28, 2020, https://inequality.org/facts/racial-inequality.
2. "Racial Economic Inequality," Inequality.org.
3. Jacob Passy, "Black Homeownership Has Declined since 2012—Here's Where Black Households Are Most Likely to Be Homeowners," MarketWatch, July 1, 2020, www.marketwatch.com/story/black-homeownership-has-declined-since-2012-heres-where-black-households-are-most-likely-to-be-homeowners-2020-06-30.
4. Rick Halpern, *Down on the Killing Floor: Black and White Workers in Chicago's Packinghouses: 1904–54* (Urbana: University of Illinois Press, 1997), 1.
5. Robin D. G. Kelley, *Hammer and Hoe: Alabama Communists during the Great Depression* (Chapel Hill: University of North Carolina Press, 2015).
6. Halpern, *Down on the Killing Floor*, 2.
7. Halpern, *Down on the Killing Floor*, 97.
8. Halpern, *Down on the Killing Floor*, 169.
9. Kelley, *Hammer and Hoe*, xxi.
10. Kelley, *Hammer and Hoe*, xxi.
11. Black Workers for Justice, "About Us," http://blackworkersforjustice.com/about-us.
12. Robin Bleiweis, "Quick Facts about the Gender Wage Gap," Center for American Progress, March 24, 2020, www.americanprogress.org/issues/women/reports/2020/03/24/482141/quick-facts-gender-wage-gap.
13. Sonam Sheth et al., "These 8 Charts Show the Glaring Gap between Men's

And Women's Salaries in the US," *Business Insider*, March 24, 2021, https://www.businessinsider.com/gender-wage-pay-gap-charts-2017-3.

14. Kim Scipes, "Social Movement Unionism or Social Justice Unionism? Disentangling Theoretical Confusion within the Global Labor Movement," *Class, Race and Corporate Power* 2, no. 3 (2014), doi.org/10.25148 /crcp.2.3.16092119.

15. Scipes, "Social Movement Unionism."

16. Max Lawson et al., "Public Good or Private Wealth?," Oxfam International, October 17, 2019, available at www.oxfam.org/en/research/public-good -or-private-wealth.

17. Yates, *Can the Working Class Change the World?*, 16.

18. Kim Scipes, *AFL-CIO's Secret War against Developing Country Workers: Solidarity or Sabotage?* (Lanham, MD: Lexington Books, 2011), 111–12.

19. Peter Dreier, "One Hundred Years Ago, Eugene Debs Gave an Anti-War Speech That Landed Him in Prison," *Common Dreams*, June 18, 2018, www.commondreams.org/views/2018/06/18/one-hundred-years-ago -eugene-debs-gave-anti-war-speech-landed-him-prison.

20. Michael Galant, "Labor Unions of the World, Unite," *Jacobin*, March 24, 2019, www.jacobinmag.com/2019/03/united-electrical-workers-ue-labor -internationalism.

21. Irving Bernstein, *The New Deal Collective Bargaining Policy* (New York: Da Capo, 1975), 182.

22. Frances Fox Piven and Richard A. Cloward, *Poor People's Movements: Why They Succeed, How They Fail* (New York: Vintage Books, 1979), 2.

23. Jeff Faux, "NAFTA, Twenty Years After: A Disaster," Economic Policy Institute, January 3, 2014, www.epi.org/blog/nafta-twenty-years-disaster.

24. Taylor E. Dark, *The Unions and the Democrats: An Enduring Alliance* (Ithaca, NY: Cornell University Press, 1999), 24.

25. Dave Jamieson and Paul Blumenthal, "Unions Spent a Record Amount on the Elections. But Not as Much as These 5 People," HuffPost, November 8, 2016, www.huffpost.com/entry/labor-union-election-2016_n_58223b92e4b0e80b 02cd7259.

Chapter 5: Class Struggle Tactics

1. Heidi Shierholz and Margaret Poydock, "Continued Surge in Strike Activity Signals Worker Dissatisfaction with Wage Growth," Economic Policy Institute, February 11, 2020, www.epi.org/publication/continued-surge-in-strike -activity.

2. Alex Gourevitch, "Gourevitch Responds to Pope," *Boston Review*, May 22, 2017, http://bostonreview.net/forum/right-strike/alex-gourevitch -gourevitch-responds-pope.

3. Ahmed White, "Workers Disarmed: The Campaign against Mass Picketing

and the Dilemma of Liberal Labor Rights," *Harvard Civil Rights–Civil Liberties Law Review* 49 (2014): 64, https://harvardcrcl.org/wp-content/uploads /sites/10/2009/06/HLC102.pdf.

4. Gourevitch, "The Right to Strike: A Radical View," *American Political Science Review* 112, no. 4 (2018): 906.

5. Ahmed White, *The Last Great Strike: Little Steel, the CIO, and the Struggle for Labor Rights in New Deal America* (Oakland: University of California Press, 2016), 167.

6. White, *Last Great Strike,* 60.

7. White, *Last Great Strike,* 57.

8. Making Change at Walmart, "Legal Notice," 2021, http://changewalmart.org /legal-notice.

9. Laurence Zuckerman, "Pilots in Sickout Told to Pay Airline $46 Million," *New York Times,* April 16, 1999, www.nytimes.com/1999/04/16/business /pilots-in-sickout-told-to-pay-airline-46-million.html.

10. Kyle Arnold, "American Airlines Wins Trial over Mechanics in Work Slowdown Case," *Dallas Morning News,* August 12, 2019, www.dallasnews.com /business/local-companies/2019/08/12/american-airlines-wins -trial-over-mechanics-in-work-slowdown-case.

11. Maxine Bernstein, "Jury Awards $93.6 Million to Former Operator of Port's Terminal 6 for Losses due to Dock Workers' Unlawful Labor Practices," Oregonlive.com, November 4, 2019, www.oregonlive.com/business /2019/11/jury-awards-936-million-to-former-operator-of-ports-terminal -6-for-losses-due-to-dock-workers-unlawful-labor-practices.html.

12. Mine Workers v. Bagwell, 512 U.S. 821 (1994).

13. Ralph Darlington and Martin Upchurch, "A Reappraisal of the Rank-and-File versus Bureaucracy Debate," *Capital & Class* 36, no. 1 (2012): 81, doi.org/10.1177/0309816811430369.

14. Darlington and Upchurch, "Reappraisal," 82.

15. Richard Hyman, *The Political Economy of Industrial Relations: Theory and Practice in a Cold Climate* (Basingstoke, UK: Macmillan, 1989), 150.

16. Ralph Darlington, *Radical Unionism: The Rise and Fall of Revolutionary Syndicalism* (Chicago: Haymarket Books, 2013), 31.

17. American Federation of Teachers, "Joining Voices: Inclusive Strategies for Labor's Renewal," 12, submitted December 2004 to the AFL-CIO, available at https://archive.org/details/JoiningVoices.

Chapter 6: Class Struggle Organizing, Rank-and-File Unionism, and the Militant Minority

1. Fletcher and Gapasin, *Solidarity Divided,* xii.

2. Stanley Aronowitz, *False Promises: The Shaping of American Working Class Consciousness* (New York: McGraw-Hill, 1973).

3. Uetricht and Eidlin, "US Union Revitalization," 40.

4. Foner, *T.U.E.L. to the End of the Gompers Era*, 122.

5. Foner, *T.U.E.L. to the End of the Gompers Era*, 131.

6. Roger Keeran, *The Communist Party and the Auto Workers' Unions* (Bloomington: Indiana University Press, 1980), 13.

7. Keeran, *Communist Party and the Auto Workers' Unions*, 118.

8. Farrell Dobbs, *Teamster Power* (New York: Monad Press, 1973), 11.

9. Uetricht and Eidlin, "US Union Revitalization," 37.

10. Charlie Post, "The Forgotten Militants," *Jacobin*, August 8, 2016, www.jacobinmag.com/2016/08/the-forgotten-militants.

11. Foner, *T.U.E.L. to the End of the Gompers Era*, 124.

12. Elbaum, *Revolution in the Air*, 100.

13. William Z. Foster, "The Principles and Program of the Trade Union Educational League," *Labor Herald* 1, no. 1 (March 1922): 5, available at www.marxists.org/history/usa/pubs/laborherald/v1n01-mar-1922-color.pdf.

14. Rick Fantasia, *Cultures of Solidarity: Consciousness, Action, and Contemporary American Workers* (Berkeley: University of California Press, 1989).

15. William Z. Foster, *Labor Herald Library*, bk. 4, *The Bankruptcy of the American Labor Movement* (Chicago: Trade Union Educational League, 1922), 24, available at www.marxists.org/history/usa/pubs/tuel/04-The%20 Bunkruptcy%20of%20American%20Labor.pdf.

16. Elizabeth Gurley Flynn, "The Truth about the Paterson Strike," speech at the New York Civic Club Forum, January 31, 1914, quoted in Ralph Darlington, *Radical Unionism: the Rise and Fall of Revolutionary Syndicalism* (Chicago: Haymarket Books, 2013), 118.

17. Elbaum, *Revolution in the Air*, 133.

18. Elbaum, *Revolution in the Air*, 133.

19. *Second Congress of the Communist International: Minutes of the Proceedings*, vol. 2 (London: New Park Publications, 1977), 167.

20. Bart Barnes, "Arnold Miller, Once Reform President of UMW, Dies at 62," *Washington Post*, July 13, 1985, www.washingtonpost.com/archive /local/1985/07/13/arnold-miller-once-reform-president-of-umw-dies -at-62/4ec87982-96e4-4ee6-8158-2d79ebfc36dd.

21. Kim Moody, "The Rank and File Strategy," *Jacobin*, August 9, 2018, www .jacobinmag.com/2018/08/unions-socialists-rank-and-file-strategy-kim-moody.

22. Steve Early, "The Enduring Legacy and Contemporary Relevance of Labor Insurgency in the 1970s," in *Rebel Rank and File: Labor Militancy and Revolt from Below in the Long 1970s*, eds. Aaron Brenner, Robert Brenner, and Calvin Winslow (London: Verso, 2010), 357–94.

23. Jasmine Kerrissey, "Teacher Strike Wave: By the Numbers," *Labor Notes*, October 4, 2018, https://labornotes.org/blogs/2018/10/teacher-strike -wave-numbers.

24. Dubofsky, *"Big Bill" Haywood*, 62.

25. Howard Kimeldorf, *Reds or Rackets? The Making of Radical and Conservative*

Unions on the Waterfront (Oakland: University of California Press, 1992), 87.

26. Jarol B. Manheim, "The Emerging Role of Worker Centers in Union Organizing: An Update and Supplement," US Chamber of Commerce (2017), 10, www.uschamber.com/sites/default/files/uscc_wfi_workercenterreport_2017.pdf.

27. Leslie C. Gates et al., "Sizing Up Worker Center Income (2008–2014): A Study of Revenue Size, Stability, and Streams," in No One Size Fits All: Worker Organization, Policy, and Movement in a New Economic Age, eds. Janice Fine et al. (Champaign, IL: Labor and Employment Relations Association, 2018), 39–65, electronic version.

28. Incite! Women of Color against Violence, ed., *The Revolution Will Not Be Funded: Beyond the Non-Profit Industrial Complex; With a New Preface and Foreword* (Durham, NC: Duke University Press, 2017).

29. Catherine L. Fisk, "Workplace Democracy and Democratic Worker Organizations: Notes on Worker Centers," *Theoretical Inquiries in Law* 17, no. 1 (February 2016): 118, doi.org/10.1515/til-2016-0005.

30. ROC United, "Board of Directors," accessed May 20, 2021, https://rocunited.org/board-of-directors.

31. Jean-Carl Elliott, "ROC Confidential," Organizing Work, October 21, 2019, https://organizing.work/2019/10/roc-confidential.

32. Jessica Bruder, "Meet the Immigrants Who Took On Amazon," *Wired*, November 12, 2019, www.wired.com/story/meet-the-immigrants-who-took-on-amazon.

33. Keeran, *Communist Party and the Auto Workers' Unions*, 12.

34. Keeran, *Communist Party and the Auto Workers' Unions*, 12.

35. Farhad Manjoo, "Abolish Billionaires," *New York Times*, February 6, 2019, www.nytimes.com/2019/02/06/opinion/abolish-billionaires-tax.html.

36. Americans for Tax Fairness, "Tale of Two Crises: Billionaires Gain as Workers Feel Pandemic Pain," May 21, 2020, https://americansfortaxfairness.org /issue/tale-two-crises-billionaires-gain-workers-feel-pandemic-pain.

37. *Forbes*, "Forbes Releases 39th Annual Forbes 400 Ranking of the Richest Americans," news release, September 8, 2020, www.forbes.com/sites/forbespr /2020/09/08/forbes-releases-39th-annual-forbes-400-ranking-of-the-richest -americans.

38. Perry Anderson, "The Limits and Possibilities of Trade Union Action," in *The Incompatibles: Trade Union Militancy and the Consensus*, eds. Robin Blackburn and Alexander Cockburn (London: Penguin, 1967), 264.

39. Anderson, "Limits and Possibilities of Trade Union Action," 264.

40. Anderson, "Limits and Possibilities of Trade Union Action," 263.

41. Melvyn Dubofsky and Joseph A. McCartin, *We Shall Be All: A History of the Industrial Workers of the World* (Urbana: University of Illinois Press, 2000), 32.

Chapter 7: Class Struggle Strategy

1. Peter Onley, "Where Did the OUR Walmart Campaign Go Wrong?," *In These Times*, December 14, 2015, https://inthesetimes.com/article/our-walmart -union-ufcw-black-friday.

2. Eileen Appelbaum, Arne Kalleberg, and Hye Jin Rho, "Nonstandard Work Arrangements and Older Americans, 2005–2017," Economic Policy Institute, February 28, 2019, www.epi.org/publication/nonstandard-work -arrangements-and-older-americans-2005-2017.

3. Mark Meinster, "How Unions Can Lay the Ground for the Next Upsurge," Labor Notes, October 15, 2020, www.labornotes.org/2020/10/how-unions -can-lay-ground-next-upsurge.

4. United Electrical, Radio and Machine Workers of America, *Them and Us Unionism* (Pittsburgh: United Electrical, Radio and Machine Workers of America, 2020), available at www.ueunion.org/ThemAndUs.

5. Kim Moody, *On New Terrain: How Capital Is Reshaping the Battleground of Class War* (Chicago: Haymarket Books, 2017), 19.

6. Joe Allen, "Studying Logistics," *Jacobin*, February 12, 2015, www.jacobinmag.com/2015/02/logistics-industry-organizing-labor.

7. Moody, *On New Terrain*, 19.

8. AFL-CIO, *AFL-CIO Commission on the Future of Work and Unions: Report to the AFL-CIO General Board*, September 13, 2019, https://aflcio.org/reports /afl-cio-commission-future-work-and-unions.

Bibliography

AFL-CIO. *AFL-CIO Commission on the Future of Work and Unions.* September 13, 2019. https://aflcio.org/reports/afl-cio-commission-future-work-and -unions.

Allen, Joe. "The Rank and File Strategy: A Resource List." Midwest Socialist, June 7, 2019. https://midwestsocialist.com/2019/06/07/the-rank-and -file-strategy-a-resource-list.

———. "Studying Logistics." *Jacobin*, December 2, 2015. www.jacobinmag.com/2015/02/logistics-industry-organizing-labor.

American Federation of Teachers. "Joining Voices: Inclusive Strategies for Labor's Renewal." AFL-CIO website, December 2004. Available at https:// archive.org/details/JoiningVoices.

Americans for Tax Fairness. "Tale of Two Crises: Billionaires Gain as Workers Feel Pandemic Pain." Accessed May 21, 2020. https://americansfortaxfairness.org/issue/tale-two-crises-billionaires -gain-workers-feel-pandemic-pain.

Anderson, Elizabeth S., and Chase Burghgrave. "Where Despots Rule." *Jacobin*, June 29, 2017. www.jacobinmag.com/2017/06/private-government -interview-elizabeth-anderson.

Anderson, Kevin B. "What Marx Understood about Slavery." *Jacobin*, May 9, 2019. www.jacobinmag.com/2019/09/slavery-united-states-civil-war-marx.

Anderson, Perry. "The Limits and Possibilities of Trade Union Action." In *The Incompatibles: Trade Union Militancy and the Consensus*, edited by Robin Blackburn and Alexander Cockburn, 263–80. London: Penguin, 1967.

Appelbaum, Eileen, Arne Kalleberg, and Hye Jin Rho. "Nonstandard Work Arrangements and Older Americans, 2005–2017." Economic Policy Institute, February 28, 2019. www.epi.org/publication/nonstandard -work-arrangements-and-older-americans-2005-2017.

Arnold, Kyle. "American Airlines Wins Trial over Mechanics in Work Slowdown Case." *Dallas Morning News*, August 20, 2019. www.dallasnews.com /business/local-companies/2019/08/12/american-airlines-wins-trial

-over-mechanics-in-work-slowdown-case.

Aronowitz, Stanley. *False Promises: The Shaping of American Working Class Consciousness.* New York: McGraw-Hill, 1973.

Atleson, James B. *Values and Assumptions in American Labor Law.* Amherst: University of Massachusetts Press, 1983.

Barnes, Bart. "Arnold Miller, Once Reform President of UMW, Dies at 62." *Washington Post,* July 13, 1985. www.washingtonpost.com/archive/local /1985/07/13/arnold-miller-once-reform-president-of-umw-dies-at-62/ 4ec87982-96e4-4ee6-8158-2d79ebfc36dd.

Bernstein, Irving. *The New Deal Collective Bargaining Policy.* New York: Da Capo, 1975.

Bernstein, Maxine. "Jury Awards $93.6 Million to Former Operator of Port's Terminal 6 for Losses Due to Dock Workers' Unlawful Labor Practices." Oregonlive.com, November 7, 2019. www.oregonlive.com/business /2019/11/jury-awards-936-million-to-former-operator-of-ports-terminal -6-for-losses-due-to-dock-workers-unlawful-labor-practices.html.

Black Workers for Justice. "About Us." Accessed January 21, 2021. http://blackworkersforjustice.com/about-us.

Bleiweis, Robin. "Quick Facts about the Gender Wage Gap." Center for American Progress, March 24, 2020. www.americanprogress.org/issues /women/reports/2020/03/24/482141/quick-facts-gender-wage-gap.

Bruder, Jessica. "Meet the Immigrants Who Took On Amazon." *Wired,* December 11, 2019. www.wired.com/story/meet-the-immigrants -who-took-on-amazon.

Burns, Joe. *Reviving the Strike: How Working People Can Regain Power and Transform America.* New York: Ig Publishing, 2011.

———. *Strike Back: Rediscovering Militant Tactics to Confront the Attack on Public Employee Unions.* New York: Ig Publishing, 2019.

———. "STRIKE! Why Mothballing Labor's Key Weapon Is Wrong." *New Labor Forum* 19, no. 2 (2010): 59–65. doi.org/10.4179/nlf.192.0000009.

Bussel, Robert. *From Harvard to the Ranks of Labor: Powers Hapgood and the American Working Class.* University Park: Pennsylvania State University Press, 1999.

Chicago Community and Workers' Rights. "About." Accessed March 2, 2019. https://chicagoworkersrights.org/about.

Chung, Heidi. "The Richest 1% Own 50% of Stocks Held by American Households." Yahoo! Finance, January 17, 2019. https://finance.yahoo .com/news/the-richest-1-own-50-of-stocks-held-by-american-households -150758595.html.

Clifford, Catherine. "The Majority of Billionaires in the World Are Self-Made." CNBC, May 10, 2019. www.cnbc.com/2019/05/10/wealthx-billionaire

-census-majority-of-worlds-billionaires-self-made.html.

Dannin, Ellen, and Ann Hodges. "Overruling the Judicial Amendments—What Is to Be Done?" *Truthout*, September 12, 2013. https://truthout.org /articles/overruling-the-judicial-amendments-what-is-to-be-done.

Dark, Taylor E. *The Unions and the Democrats: An Enduring Alliance*. Ithaca: Cornell University Press, 1999.

Darlington, Ralph. *Radical Unionism: The Rise and Fall of Revolutionary Syndicalism*. Chicago: Haymarket Books, 2013.

———. *Syndicalism and the Transition to Communism: An International Comparative Analysis*. Chicago: Haymarket Books, 2013.

Darlington, Ralph, and Martin Upchurch. "A Reappraisal of the Rank-and-File versus Bureaucracy Debate." *Capital & Class* 36, no. 1 (2012): 77–95. doi.org/10.1177/0309816811430369.

De Caux, Len. *Labor Radical: From the Wobblies to CIO; A Personal History*. Boston: Beacon Press, 1971.

Dilawar, Arvind. "Amazon Is the Best Argument against Capitalism." *Pacific Standard*, February 7, 2019. https://psmag.com/ideas/amazon-is-the -best-argument-against-capitalism.

Dimick, Matthew. "Labor Rights Will Not Save the Labor Movement." *Jacobin*, December 12, 2019. www.jacobinmag.com/2019/12/labor-rights -movement-freedom-nlra-nlrb-mass-picketing.

Dobbs, Farrell. *Teamster Power*. New York: Monad Press, 1973.

Dolan, Kerry. "The Forbes 400: The Definitive Ranking of the Wealthiest Americans in 2020." *Forbes*, September 8, 2020. www.forbes.com/forbes-400.

Domhoff, G. William. "Power in America: Wealth, Income, and Power." WhoRulesAmerica.net. Last modified April 2017. https://whorulesamerica.ucsc.edu/power/wealth.html.

Draper, Hal. "The Principle of Self-Emancipation in Marx and Engels." *Socialist Register* 8, March 1971.

———. "Why the Working Class Is the Key to Progress." In Introduction to Independent Socialism, 60–64. 2nd ed. Berkeley, CA: Independent Socialist Press, 1970. Available at https://www.marxists.org/history/etol/ document/is-us/IS-documents/70-72/70-(5).pdf.

Dreier, Peter. "One Hundred Years Ago, Eugene Debs Gave an Anti-War Speech That Landed Him in Prison." *Common Dreams*, June 18, 2018. www.commondreams.org/views/2018/06/18/one-hundred-years -ago-eugene-debs-gave-anti-war-speech-landed-him-prison.

Dubofsky, Melvyn. *"Big Bill" Haywood*. New York: St. Martin's, 1987.

Dubofsky, Melvyn, and Joseph A. McCartin. *We Shall Be All: A History of the Industrial Workers of the World*. Urbana: University of Illinois Press, 2000.

Early, Steve. *The Civil Wars in US Labor: Birth of a New Workers' Movement or Death Throes of the Old?* Chicago: Haymarket Books, 2011.

———. "The Enduring Legacy and Contemporary Relevance of Labor Insurgency in the 1970s." In *Rebel Rank and File: Labor Militancy and Revolt from below in the Long 1970s*, edited by Aaron Brenner, Robert Brenner, and Calvin Winslow, 357–94. London: Verso, 2010.

Elbaum, Max. *Revolution in the Air: Sixties Radicals Turn to Lenin, Mao and Che.* London: Verso, 2018.

Elliott, Jean-Carl. "ROC Confidential." Organizing Work, October 21, 2019. https://organizing.work/2019/10/roc-confidential.

Fantasia, Rick. *Cultures of Solidarity: Consciousness, Action, and Contemporary American Workers.* Berkeley: University of California Press, 2012.

Faux, Jeff. "NAFTA, Twenty Years After: A Disaster." Economic Policy Institute, January 23, 2014. www.epi.org/blog/nafta-twenty-years-disaster.

Fisk, Catherine L. "Workplace Democracy and Democratic Worker Organizations: Notes on Worker Centers." *Theoretical Inquiries in Law* 17, no. 1 (2016). doi.org/10.1515/til-2016-0005.

Fletcher, Bill, and Fernando Gapasin. *Solidarity Divided: The Crisis in Organized Labor and a New Path toward Social Justice.* Berkeley: University of California Press, 2009.

Foner, Philip S. *The T.U.E.L. to the End of the Gompers Era.* Vol. 9 of *History of the Labor Movement in the United States.* New York: International Publishers, 1991.

Forbes. "Forbes Releases 39th Annual Forbes 400 Ranking of the Richest Americans" (news release). September 9, 2020. www.forbes.com/sites /forbespr/2020/09/08/forbes-releases-39th-annual-forbes-400-ranking -of-the-richest-americans.

Foster, William Z. *The Bankruptcy of the American Labor Movement.* Book 4 of *Labor Herald Library.* Chicago: Trade Union Educational League, 1922. Available at www.marxists.org/history/usa/unions/tuel/1922/1000 -foster-bankruptcy.pdf.

———. *Misleaders of Labor.* New York: Trade Union Education League, 1927.

———. "The Principles and Program of the Trade Union Educational League." *Labor Herald* 1, no. 1 (March 1922). Available at www.marxists.org /archive/foster/1922/principles.htm.

Galant, Michael. "Labor Unions of the World, Unite." *Jacobin*, March 24, 2019. www.jacobinmag.com/2019/03/united-electrical-workers-ue-labor -internationalism.

Gates, Leslie C. et al. "Sizing Up Worker Center Income (2008–2014): A Study of Revenue Size, Stability, and Streams." In *No One Size Fits All: Worker Organization, Policy, and Movement in a New Economic Age*, edited by Janice Fine et al., 39–65 (electronic version). Champaign, IL: Labor and

Employment Relations Association, 2018.

Geoghegan, Thomas. *Which Side Are You On? Trying to Be for Labor When It's Flat on Its Back*. New York: New Press, 2004.

Gilpin, Toni. *Long Deep Grudge: A Story of Big Capital, Radical Labor, and Class War in the American Heartland*. Chicago: Haymarket Books, 2020.

Gordon, Colin. "The Coronavirus Wouldn't Be Decimating Meatpacking Plants if Company Bosses Hadn't Busted the Unions." *Jacobin*, May 18, 2020. www.jacobinmag.com/2020/05/iowa-upwa-meat-processing-unons -packinghouse-coronavirus.

Gourevitch, Alex. "Gourevitch Responds to Pope." *Boston Review*, May 22, 2017. http://bostonreview.net/forum/right-strike/alex-gourevitch-gourevitch -responds-pope.

———. "A Radical Defense of the Right to Strike." *Jacobin*, December 7, 2018. www.jacobinmag.com/2018/07/right-to-strike-freedom-civil -liberties-oppression.

Halpern, Rick. *Down on the Killing Floor: Black and White Workers in Chicago's Packinghouses: 1904–54*. Urbana: University of Illinois Press, 1997.

Hoxie, Robert F. "Trade Unionism in the United States: The Essence of Unionism and the Interpretation of Union Types." *Journal of Political Economy* 22, no. 5 (May 1914): 464–81. doi.org/10.1086/252455.

Hyman, Richard. *The Political Economy of Industrial Relations: Theory and Practice in a Cold Climate*. Basingstoke, UK: Macmillan, 1989.

Incite!: Women of Color against Violence, ed. *The Revolution Will Not Be Funded: Beyond the Non-Profit Industrial Complex: With a New Preface and Foreword*. Durham, NC: Duke University Press, 2017.

Jamieson, Dave, and Paul Blumenthal. "Unions Spent a Record Amount on the Elections. But Not as Much as These 5 People." HuffPost, November 8, 2016. www.huffpost.com/entry/labor-union-election-2016_n _58223b92e4b0e80b02cd7259.

Jones, A. C. "UAW Rank-and-File Opposition." In *Rebel Rank and File: Labor Militancy and Revolt from below in the Long 1970s*, edited by Aaron Brenner, Robert Brenner, and Calvin Winslow, 281–310. London: Verso, 2010.

Keeran, Roger. *The Communist Party and the Auto Workers' Unions*. Bloomington: Indiana University Press, 1980.

Kelley, Robin D. G. *Hammer and Hoe: Alabama Communists during the Great Depression*. Chapel Hill: University of North Carolina Press, 2015.

Kerrissey, Jasmine. "Teacher Strike Wave: By the Numbers." Labor Notes, October 4, 2018. https://labornotes.org/blogs/2018/10/teacher-strike-wave-numbers.

Kimeldorf, Howard. *Reds or Rackets? The Making of Radical and Conservative Unions on the Waterfront*. Oakland: University of California Press, 1992.

Kolin, Andrew. *Political Economy of Labor Repression in the United States*.

Lanham, MD: Lexington Books, 2018.

Laney, Tom. "Interview with Solidarity Unionist Tom Laney." *Solidarity Review*, February 16, 2018. www.solidarityreview.com/latestnews/tomlaneyinterview.

Lawson, Max, and Man-Kwun Chan. "Public Good or Private Wealth?" Oxfam International, October 17, 2019. www.oxfam.org/en/research/public -good-or-private-wealth.

Making Change at Walmart. "Legal Notice," 2014. http://changewalmart.org /legal-notice.

Manheim, Jarol. "The Emerging Role of Worker Centers: An Update." US Chamber of Commerce, March 15, 2018. www.uschamber.com/sites /default/files/uscc_wfi_workercenterreport_2017.pdf.

Manjoo, Farhad. "Abolish Billionaires." *New York Times*, February 6, 2019. www.nytimes.com/2019/02/06/opinion/abolish-billionaires-tax.html.

Marx, Karl. "General Rules, October 1864." International Workingmen's Association, 1864. Available at www.marxists.org/history/international /iwma/documents/1864/rules.htm.

Marx, Karl, and Eleanor Marx Aveling. *Value, Price, and Profit*. Chicago: Charles H. Kerr & Co., 1910.

Matles, James J., and James Higgins. *Them and Us: Struggles of a Rank-and-File Union*. Pittsburgh: United Electrical. Radio and Machine Workers of America, 1995.

Meinster, Mark. "How Unions Can Lay the Ground for the Next Upsurge." Labor Notes, October 15, 2020. www.labornotes.org/2020/10/how-unions -can-lay-ground-next-upsurge.

Mine Workers v. Bagwell, 512 U.S. 821 (1994).

Moody, Kim. *On New Terrain: How Capital Is Reshaping the Battleground of Class War*. Chicago: Haymarket Books, 2018.

———. "The Rank and File Strategy." *Jacobin*, September 8, 2018. www.jacobinmag.com/2018/08/unions-socialists-rank-and-file -strategy-kim-moody.

Needleman, Ruth. *Black Freedom Fighters in Steel: The Struggle for Democratic Unionism*. Ithaca: ILR Press, 2003.

Onley, Peter. "Where Did the OUR Walmart Campaign Go Wrong?" *In These Times*, December 14, 2015. https://inthesetimes.com/article/our-walmart -union-ufcw-black-friday.

Parenti, Michael. *Democracy for the Few*. Boston: Wadsworth Cengage Learning, 2008.

Passy, Jacob. "Black Homeownership Has Declined since 2012—Here's Where Black Households Are Most Likely to Be Homeowners." MarketWatch, July 1, 2020. www.marketwatch.com/story/black-homeownership-has -declined-since-2012-heres-where-black-households-are-most-likely-to

-be-homeowners-2020-06-30.

Peterson, Florence. "Analysis of Strike in 1937." United States Bureau of Labor Statistics, 1938. https://www.bls.gov/wsp/publications/annual -summaries/pdf/analysis-of-strikes-in-1937.pdf.

Piketty, Thomas. *Capital in the Twenty-First Century*. Cambridge, MA: Belknap Press of Harvard University Press, 2017.

Piven, Frances Fox, and Richard A. Cloward. *Poor People's Movements: Why They Succeed, How They Fail*. New York: Vintage Books, 1979.

Post, Charlie. "The Forgotten Militants." *Jacobin*, August 8, 2016. www.jacobinmag.com/2016/08/the-forgotten-militants.

"Racial Economic Inequality." Inequality.org, August 28, 2020. https://inequality.org/facts/racial-inequality.

ROC United. "Board of Directors." Accessed May 20, 2021. https://rocunited.org/board-of-directors.

Ross, Stephanie. "Varieties of Social Unionism: Towards A Framework for Comparison." *Just Labour* 11 (Autumn 2007): 16–34. doi.org/10.25071/1705-1436.84.

Sanders, Bernie. "It's Time to Complete the Revolution We Started." *Guardian*, February 25, 2019. www.theguardian.com/commentisfree/2019/feb/25 /its-time-to-complete-the-revolution-we-started.

Scipes, Kim. *AFL-CIO's Secret War against Developing Country Workers: Solidarity or Sabotage?* Lanham, MD: Lexington Books, 2011.

———. "Social Movement Unionism or Social Justice Unionism? Disentangling Theoretical Confusion within the Global Labor Movement." *Class Race Corporate Power* 2, no. 3 (2014). doi.org/10.25148/crcp.2.3.16092119.

Shierholz, Heidi, and Margaret Poydock. "Continued Surge in Strike Activity Signals Worker Dissatisfaction with Wage Growth." Economic Policy Institute, February 11, 2020. www.epi.org/publication/continued-surge -in-strike-activity.

Stepan-Norris, Judith, and Maurice Zeitlin. *Left Out: Reds and America's Industrial Unions*. Cambridge, UK: Cambridge University Press, 2005.

Stern, Andy. *A Country That Works: Getting America Back on Track*. New York: Free Press, 2008.

Taft, Philip. "On the Origins of Business Unionism." *Industrial and Labor Relations Review* 17, no. 1 (October 1963): 20–38. doi.org/10.2307/2520883.

Thompson, Frederick, and Patrick Murfin. *The I.W.W.: Its First Seventy Years (1905–1975); The History of an Effort to Organize the Working Class*. Chicago: Industrial Workers of the World, 1976.

Uetricht, Micah, and Barry Eidlin. "US Union Revitalization and the Missing 'Militant Minority.'" *Labor Studies Journal* 44, no. 1 (March 2019): 36–59. doi.org/10.1177/0160449x19828470.

United Electrical, Radio and Machine Workers of America. *Them and Us Unionism*. Pittsburgh: United Electrical, Radio and Machine Workers of America, 2020. Available at www.ueunion.org/ThemAndUs.

Weinstein, James. *The Corporate Ideal in the Liberal State: 1900–1918*. Boston: Beacon Press, 1968.

White, Ahmed. *The Last Great Strike: Little Steel, the CIO, and the Struggle for Labor Rights in New Deal America*. Oakland: University of California Press, 2016.

———. "Workers Disarmed: The Campaign against Mass Picketing and the Dilemma of Liberal Labor Rights." *Harvard Civil Rights Law Review* 49 (2014): 59–121. https://harvardcrcl.org/wp-content/uploads /sites/10/2009/06/HLC102.pdf.

Workers Lab. "2019 Year in Review." January 2020. www.theworkerslab.com /blog/end-of-year-report.

Yates, Michael. *Can the Working Class Change the World?* New York: Monthly Review Press, 2018.

———. *The Great Inequality*. New York: Routledge, 2016.

Zinn Education Project. "Sept. 26, 1909: International Ladies' Garment Workers' Union Strike." Accessed September 8, 2020. www.zinnedproject.org/news/tdih/ILGWU-strike.

Zuckerman, Laurence. "Pilots in Sickout Told to Pay Airline $46 Million." *New York Times*, April 16, 1999. www.nytimes.com/1999/04/16/business /pilots-in-sickout-told-to-pay-airline-46-million.html.

Index

About the Author

Joe Burns is a veteran union negotiator and labor lawyer with over twenty-five years' experience negotiating labor agreements. He is currently the Director of Collective Bargaining for the Association of Flight Attendants, CWA. He graduated from the New York University School of Law. Prior to law school he worked in a public sector hospital and was president of his AFSCME Local. He is the author of *Strike Back: Rediscovering Militant Tactics to Fight the Attacks on Public Employee Unions* and *Reviving the Strike: How Working People Can Regain Power and Transform America*.

About Haymarket Books

Haymarket Books is a radical, independent, nonprofit book publisher based in Chicago. Our mission is to publish books that contribute to struggles for social and economic justice. We strive to make our books a vibrant and organic part of social movements and the education and development of a critical, engaged, international left.

We take inspiration and courage from our namesakes, the Haymarket martyrs, who gave their lives fighting for a better world. Their 1886 struggle for the eight-hour day—which gave us May Day, the international workers' holiday—reminds workers around the world that ordinary people can organize and struggle for their own liberation. These struggles continue today across the globe—struggles against oppression, exploitation, poverty, and war.

Since our founding in 2001, Haymarket Books has published more than five hundred titles. Radically independent, we seek to drive a wedge into the risk-averse world of corporate book publishing. Our authors include Noam Chomsky, Arundhati Roy, Rebecca Solnit, Angela Y. Davis, Howard Zinn, Amy Goodman, Wallace Shawn, Mike Davis, Winona LaDuke, Ilan Pappé, Richard Wolff, Dave Zirin, Keeanga-Yamahtta Taylor, Nick Turse, Dahr Jamail, David Barsamian, Elizabeth Laird, Amira Hass, Mark Steel, Avi Lewis, Naomi Klein, and Neil Davidson. We are also the trade publishers of the acclaimed Historical Materialism Book Series and of Dispatch Books.

Also Available from Haymarket Books

*Disposable Domestics: Immigrant Women Workers
in the Global Economy*
Grace Chang, foreword by Alicia Garza, afterword by Ai-jen Poo

Dying for an iPhone: Apple, Foxconn, and The Lives of China's Workers
Jenny Chan, Pun Ngai, and Mark Selden

*The Long Deep Grudge: A Story of Big Capital, Radical Labor,
and Class War in the American Heartland*
Toni Gilpin

*On New Terrain: How Capital is Reshaping
the Battleground of Class War*
Kim Moody

The Package King: A Rank and File History of UPS
Joe Allen

Poor Workers' Unions: Rebuilding Labor from Below
Vanessa Tait, foreword by Bill Fletcher, afterword by Cristina
Tzintzún

*Radicals in the Barrio: Magonistas, Socialists, Wobblies,
and Communists in the Mexican-American Working Class*
Justin Akers Chacón

Rank and File: Personal Histories by Working-Class Organizers
Alice and Staughton Lynd